Don't Eat The Cat

– MARGARET WALKER –

To my dear sister, Beryl.

FASTPRINT PUBLISHING
PETERBOROUGH, ENGLAND

DON'T EAT THE CAT
Copyright © Margaret Walker 2009

ISBN 978-184426-623-4

First Published 2009 by
FASTPRINT PUBLISHING
Peterborough, England.

Mixed Sources
Product group from well-managed
forests, and other controlled sources
www.fsc.org Cert no. TT-COC-002641
© 1996 Forest Stewardship Council
FSC

The wood used to produce the paper used in this book comes from
well managed forests, independently certified in accordance with the
rules of the Forest Stewardship Council.

Printed by
www.printondemand-worldwide.com

Acknowledgements

To Michael, my patient and loving husband,
for his contributions to this book
and for replenishing me with cups of tea and chocolate.

To my children, Christopher, Pauline and Rosie
for allowing me to include them in yet another book

To Simon Potter, publishing editor
for his friendly and efficient help,
and to my friend Gwynn Jones of Porthmadog
for the front cover photograph.

Chapter One

'You damned parrot!' I screamed, as the wretched bird took a piece out of my left leg when I was trying to cross the busy main road near Halifax town centre. Weaving between cars and lorries was not helped by stinging hailstones and an uncontrollable yappy terrier who had wound his lead round my right leg.

I was carrying out an act of charity, such as vicars' wives are apt to be called on to perform. The owner of the damned parrot (actually I found out later it was a cockatiel) and the yappy terrier was Miss Picket, a highly-strung lady who periodically had to go into hospital for treatment for her 'nerves'. My vicar-husband, Michael, had misguidedly once offered to take her dog into kennels during her hospital stays. On two occasions this dog ferrying coincided with the first journey undertaken in our new car. Not for us that opulent new car smell, or the pristine sheets of paper in the foot wells. The unfortunate canine, unused to cars, deposited his messy offering within two minutes of the journey's start. The paper was put to good use, and the new car smell was displaced. On our third mission of mercy Miss Picket added an extra errand. As well as taking the dog to kennels she asked us to take her newly acquired bird to the pet shop. She assured us that the shopkeeper had intimated that he would 'be happy to look after it'. So I was dropped off in a hailstorm to hand it over.

As I smiled weakly at the patient lorry-driver waving me across the road with my menagerie, I extricated my right leg from the tangled lead, admonished the dog, held the birdcage out of further pecking distance of my left leg and splashed my way into the pet shop. The dog leapt up at a newly delivered bag of dog treats as I plonked the cage down on the counter.

'That's not Miss Picket's cockatiel, is it? I'm not having that bloody bird here.'

The shopkeeper's venom did not tally with the response Miss Picket had predicted.

I was shocked at his swearing. He'd only had that bird on his counter for one minute. I had a real bloody leg, and I'd managed only a 'damned', and that was strong language for a vicar's wife!

I prayed hard that the hail and traffic would stop as I proceeded to re-cross the busy road to deliver the news that it seemed we were going to have a cockatiel to stay with us indefinitely. As Michael drove the dithering dog to kennels I had vainly thought that they might take the bird as well. No such luck – and no luck either on the back seat of the car. The dog's aim had not been good.

I deposited the cockatiel on the dining room table. Sheba, our Golden Labrador, was intrigued by this shrieking bird that was intent on performing a biopsy on her inquisitive nose. Sheba's howls sent the bird into a state of apoplectic rage and I swiftly moved the cage onto a very high windowsill, well out of any battle zone. It was six weeks before Sheba was safe in the dining room; every time she had gone in, the bird had taken great delight in spitting out his sunflower seeds onto her head and then gloating with a high pitched shriek. No wonder Miss Picket's nerves were bad. Was there any room in the next hospital bed for Michael and me?

I know that the Good Samaritan had to stop on a dangerous road, and that he was good with his medical care and generous in accommodating the beaten man in the wayside inn, but how would he have coped with incontinent dogs, and leg-biting, seed-ejecting parrots? Probably better than me! However I took comfort in the fact that Miss Picket's dog was well into its teens. Next stop – the library – to find a reference book on the life expectancy of cockatiels. It was not good news!

★★★★★★★★★★★★★★★

Michael had not grown up with pets, apart from a rabbit, which his father had grudgingly allowed him to keep in the immediate post-war years. For me, rabbits were vital wartime food which my mother had try to pass off as chicken, until the day I caught her tearing out the innards of a long-eared, bob-tailed friend. Nothing was wasted. A lady in the Beverley Townswomen's Guild made brooches from rabbit paws and fur gloves from the pelts, while her husband commandeered the fluffy tails for pollinating his tomatoes. Our family consumed the rest in the form of stews and rabbit pies.

While Michael was collecting food for his rabbit that lived in a hutch in the vicarage garden at Morley, in West

Yorkshire, I was living in East Yorkshire, stroking my first pet, Sandy, a handsome ginger tom. This hungry cat had sensibly found his way to the fish oil factory in Hull, where my sister worked as a secretary. I am not sure whether my father appreciated this addition to our family. He, like Michael's father, tolerated animals rather than delighted in them. We lived behind my father's corner shop, with 'Hubert Jefferson, Tailor and Outfitter' emblazoned above both shop windows. Sandy soon discovered that the shop windows were real suntraps, and even better, that there was always a pile of interlock vests or knickers on which to make his bed. Despite being poked out of the window with father's yardstick and bustled into the back room with death-threats ringing in his ears, he lived with us through the dark years of the war.

One day I returned from school to an animal-less house. Sandy had died. I did not question where he had gone. All was to be revealed. Meat was still scarce and rationing was in force. Yes, we ate rabbit and fish, but had meagre amounts of meat. Usually we had a bread and butter tea at five o'clock, then a bowl of cornflakes and cup of Ovaltine at bedtime. It was a surprise, therefore, that one evening the gate-legged table was opened out fully, encased in a white linen cloth, and the best silver cutlery unearthed from its rosewood canteen, which lived under the sideboard. The shop was shut, the shutters were up and the blackout curtains, which mother had brightened with orange braid, were tightly drawn. Father arrived at the back door with his air raid warden friends in dark blue uniforms and they sat down round the table, while my sister Beryl, brother Barry and I sat on the settee with waiting plates.

Father went upstairs and came down with a heavily filled pillowcase, while mother sharpened the carving knife. I stared in grim fascination as mother undid the drawstring that she had sewn round the pillowcase from which she produced a huge piece of pink cooked meat. Everyone except me tucked in to this rare treat with enthusiasm. I ran upstairs in tears. How could they enjoy eating Sandy?

Of course mother came up to see what was the matter.
'Don't eat the cat!' I screamed.
'Please don't let them eat the cat!'
I couldn't understand why mother found this so funny, but when she had stopped laughing she gave me a cuddle, and told me that this pink meat was ham. (Years later I learned that it was from father's cousin's farm on Flamborough Head.) It was my family's one and only undercover wartime act, but I never understood why it had to be kept secret, and why the ham was replaced in its security pillowcase bag and hung on the top of the banister rail, only to be brought out under the cover of shuttered darkness. Father's friends whispered something about 'black market'. I couldn't think whereabouts in Beverley there was a black market, but wherever this pink meat was from, it tasted delicious, and I was mightily relieved that it was from a pig, and not from our pet cat.

Mother later told me that she had buried Sandy in the tiny patch of garden at the bottom of our backyard. I never knew exactly where, but next spring I was digging with my little trowel in readiness to plant some Virginian Stock. The soil was crumbly and black, but my next plunge of the trowel brought up lots of white crystals. Now I knew for certain where Sandy had been laid to rest.

For years – yes until I was in my teens – I honestly believed that, when cats died, their bodies, like Lot's wife, turned into salt. It was only when my parents were recounting their war memories and re-telling the story of the night-time feast, that it slipped out that they had not wanted to be caught in possession of illicit ham, and so had buried its tell-tale salt in the garden.

★★★★★★★★★★★★★★★

Apart from the rabbit stews and occasional illicit ham I ate lots of fresh vegetables from the allotment where father 'dug for victory'. Luckily he grew many rows of potatoes, so I was spared eating what I endured at my friend's house – POM – an unnatural yellow powder that was mixed with water and milk to make an unconvincing imitation of mash.

In autumn we scoured the hedgerows for brambles to make into puddings and for rose hips to make syrup. Eggs were at a premium and had to be 'put down' in an enamel pail in intriguing liquid called isinglass. The alternative was dried egg powder, which came in waxed brown cartons, and did make into surprisingly tasty scrambled egg.

Bread was available, and although looking grey and tired, it was, in fact, full of healthy additives. For most of the week we had thinly spread margarine, but on Thursday teatime (father's half day when he closed the shop and did further digging for victory) and on Sunday before evensong, we had our weekly ration of best butter. I never tasted worst butter – I wonder where that went? All things considered I reckon that my generation had a healthy start, what with sweets 'on the ration', a low fat diet, fruit from the fields, rabbit, fish and plenty of milk. We children had rather tart, but pleasant orange juice, to supplement our vitamin C, and the rather more unpleasant cod liver oil, for our vitamins A and D. On most mornings I also had an unpalatable spoonful of Californian Syrup of Figs. I suffered this, because I was very anxious not to get 'the big C'. Grown-ups talked in hushed tones about how this was a killer. It was obviously extremely important not to get it.

Every teatime my mother would interrogate each of us in turn. 'Have you been today?'

If I hadn't, I could tell a fib and then I'd worry all night whether I'd survive another week or even another day. Or else I could confess that I hadn't been, and I would then have to suffer the torture of Californian Syrup of Figs, or worse still Beecham's pills, which looked and tasted like iron ball bearings. Why couldn't I have Andrews Liver Salts like my friend Pam? They frothed up and over the glass and if drunk quickly tasted like lemonade. Well, almost. I remember a spoof rendition of the Andrews advert, which was 'Do you wake up in the morning feeling as though the bottom's dropped out of your world? Take Andrews, and you'll feel as though the world has dropped out of your bottom!'

For me, however, Andrews was not an option. It was Beecham's pills or syrup of figs. The lesser of the two evils in our household was undoubtedly the syrup of figs which mother poured out onto an old dented tablespoon. As it made its inexorable approach to my lips I closed my eyes, gulped it down and immediately stuffed my mouth with bread and jam. As for the terrible Beecham's pills alternative, well they were all right as long as you could swallow pills. I never could. Even now aspirins have to be crushed between two teaspoons and camouflaged with jam. Have you ever tried crushing a Beecham's pill? I wouldn't bother. It's almost impossible. They were so tiny and so hard that they resisted crushing and instead catapulted out of their spoon vice onto the floor. There was then nothing for it but to try to swallow the wretched bullet, now devoid of half its sugar coating, and exposing its dark grey, steely poison.

The taste stayed on your tongue for longer than the syrup of figs, and sickly sweet golden syrup was the first line of attack to get rid of it. Surely there must be a better, more tasteful way of 'keeping regular'. I resolved to find out.

When I was tall enough I found I could balance on the music stool and reach the high shelf under the stairs. It was our only bookshelf. They didn't print many books in the war; the pages were coffee coloured and rough, the print was minute and the lines were close together. I can remember exactly that books we had: a Chambers Dictionary with a blue, worn spine, A Children's Everything Within, which had useful things like Morse code, how to write in secret ink and how to make a paper plane; Arthur Mee's Children's Encyclopaedia from which I tried to learn French; a grey fat needlework book which failed to enthuse me with a desire to herring bone, and a decrepit Mrs Beeton's Book of Household Management, which exhorted you to take 18 pullets' eggs and do degree level origami with starched napkins.

Next to these reference books were my three prizes: *Cheeky Brown,* a thin yellow book about a baby chicken - my Sunday school prize in1946; *Jan at Island School,* a school

English Prize and *Two girls from the West,* my arithmetic prize. These travelled with me to college and to homes in Yorkshire and Wales until they found their retirement home on the bookshelves of a charity shop. Maybe someone will now know what the two girls from the west got up to. I never progressed beyond page two.

And now for the last book – that is, as in Desert Island Discs, besides the Bible and Shakespeare. It stood on the shelf, stout and imposing, and between its dark maroon, leather bound cover was hidden a host of medical mysteries. It was to this book I turned from my precarious stance on the music stool. I had already decided on my strategy. Should anyone come into the room unexpectedly I would push it back quickly and pretend I was looking for the Bible. They couldn't be cross about that.

I was entranced by the pictures of skeletons and skinless muscular torsos, and mesmerised by the interminable length of intestines packed into what I now knew was called the abdomen. But I had to pursue my research and save the pictures for another day. I nearly didn't get as far as the big C. so interested was I in abortion. I read on through abscesses and acne and decided early on that anaemia was not a good thing to get. Apparently the remedy is to eat iron. That was not good news. However I gathered that chocolate has iron in it. Therefore I must eat chocolate. Which maxim I have tried to live up to.

Baldness didn't interest me, but breasts did. Bronchitis I knew about, but bulimia was new to me and sounded horrid – fancy wanting to make yourself sick! So I skipped on through the C's – past cancer and cirrhosis, and eventually arrived at the page itself. Here was 'the big C'.

Now I would never have to get embarrassed and ask my mother what constipation was.

I read on avidly. No wonder my mother was anxious. It could cause anal fissures. I would have to go back to the 'A's to see what they were. They sounded bad.

No wonder we all suffered – we had no oranges in the war. How come syrup of figs was always available though? I learned some interesting new words like laxatives and purgatives. Help! I must keep regular or I'll end up with my mum pushing pessaries up my bottom. But before I could pull down the Chambers dictionary and find out what awful things pessaries might be, my research was aborted. My dad had come in to report that Mr Holland across the road had died (whispered tones) – of the big C.

I wasn't supposed to hear this last bit. But it didn't matter. I now knew. And just to be on the safe side I had a second helping of prunes for pudding.

Chapter Two

After Sandy had died (and turned into salt!) my sister brought home a tortoiseshell kitten, which she named Figaro. My father was not amused. However, thinking that he could soon train this little cat not to sit in his shop window, he capitulated, on the understanding that its name be changed. He was not prepared to stand in the street in Mozart opera mode calling 'Figaro, Figaro'. So Figaro became Frisky, and Frisky soon learned where the best sunspot was, and this was important, as the year was 1947. There may have been colder winters since, but the 1947 winter was memorably long. Between pavement and road stood gigantic piles of snow, which became increasingly grey and gritty until it finally melted in April. Walking to school, as a seven-year old, I often cried when the snow came over the top of my wellies, and the ice chafed my legs where the boots rubbed.

I am fortunate in having a strong bladder, which I probably developed from never wanting to cross the icy playground to reach the miniscule outside school toilets. They had no roof, and, if you felt you needed it, you had to ask teacher, in front of all the class, for the required number of sheets of toilet paper. The shame of letting all your fellow pupils know that you needed to do 'a big job' was not as great as the discomfort felt when applying these hard-won sheets of paper. Not the soft, silky aloe vera ones we enjoy today, but flimsy, tissue-thin, crackly bottom-scratching sheets, which rejoiced in the name of Izal Medicated toilet paper. Its absorbability rating was nil. Its smearing ability was 10 out of 10. Its only redeeming features were its healthy carbolic smell and its use as tracing paper. I suppose, too, that it was marginally better than the torn off squares of newspaper strung on coarse string in my grandparents' outside earth closet. At least Izal didn't smear black printing ink onto my nether regions!

We were expected to play outside at playtime, whatever the weather. First we had to pick up a straw and drink our bottle of milk. This third of a pint cost two and a half pence a week when I started school, but became free a few months later. In winter it froze in its crates and popped the cardboard tops off like little hats, on columns of ice shards. In summer the milk stood out in the sun, producing sick-making curds that clogged up the flimsy paper straws. The milk was often tipped away when teacher wasn't looking, but we did keep the cardboard bottle tops with a punched out hole in the middle. They smelt vile even when you had washed off the soured cream, but were just the right size for making pom-poms for your pixie hood by putting two together, back to back, and winding wool round and round, then inserting wool between the tops, pulling tight and knotting, and finally cutting the outside loops and tearing out the soggy cardboard.

Playground games altered with the season: whips and tops, marbles, conkers, hopscotch, and skipping – none of which was subject to 'Health and Safety' laws. We made long icy slides all the way from the door to the school gate, onto which the spoilsport school caretaker would throw clinker from the evil smelling boiler. We formed gangs, joining arms in a long line as though we were going to dance the 'Palais Glide' and chanted terrifying threats to our opponents: 'Anybody in the way gets a good kick'. Hardly the ethos of a church school, which it was!

Slates were just giving way to scratchy pens and ink, and reading started with *Old Lob, book one.* I can't remember whether Lob was a horse or a cow – or maybe he was the farmer? Anyway I soon learned to read, to recite my tables, and to memorise the Lord's Prayer and the Apostles' Creed. Every Good Friday I still recall my infant school days when I sat in the back desk and listened entranced to the story of the crucifixion, read by Miss Taylor in top class. Jesus's beatings were so cruel and unjust, that I sobbed until tears trickled down my sloping desk, and I sniffed until Adrian Middleton lent me his grubby hanky. Many years later, on hearing of Adrian's untimely death, I wept again, but will continue to remember both his seven-year old good looks and his kindness.

We were placed in the classroom in order of merit, according to our skills in the three 'R's. Adrian must have slipped down the pecking order later that year, so I had to sit next to a pale, gawky boy with horn-rimmed glasses – Robert Fairbairn who shared honours with me in arithmetic and English, and who was made to play piano duets with me at the Sunday school party. His only virtue was that he was equally as bad as I was at craft. When *Beacon Reader book 2* and joined up writing gave way to craft it was a mercy for the less academic children. For Robert and for me it was torture. There were three craft activities: knitting, raffia and clay. We had no choice, but I prayed that Miss Taylor would let me knit. My mother had taught me to knit when I was four, to keep me quiet at British and Foreign Bible Society meetings.

Row one, however, was given raffia work. Wouldn't you have thought there might have been a raffia shortage in the war? No such luck. So I was armed with a bendy khaki disc of cardboard with a circle cut in the middle. Around this I had to wind and buttonhole yards of purple raffia to make a tablemat. By week one I had managed to splinter my raffia into straggly strands and by week two had got the whole thing into such a mess that I prodded it feverishly with my long needle, producing irretrievable knots. Miss Taylor was not impressed, and held it up at the end of the lesson to show class four how not to make a mat. Tears of mortification welled up in my eyes and I started to plan its demise.

Instead of putting it into the craft bag on teacher's desk, I hid it down my navy knickers until, on my way from school, in the secrecy of the allotments I took out the offending scratchy article and ran home. The fire was burning brightly in the black Yorkist range, where the old sooty kettle was puffing and spurting in anticipation of tea. The mat went up in a flurry of yellow and green hissing flames in a satisfying cremation.

Next week's craft lesson and, - 'Margaret Jefferson, where is your mat?'

'Don't know, Miss Taylor' I lied. 'Ashes to ashes and dust to dust' would have been the honourable answer.

'Well for this week you'll have to get on with something else.' (Please God let it be knitting.)

'You can do clay' said Miss Taylor. God was having his revenge.

Even worse than knotty, splitting raffia was the thought of putting my hands into horrid cold wet clay.

I hated it then. I hate it now. Clay at infants' school, clay on my father's allotment, clay in our first vicarage garden – slimy yellow ochre when wet; hard unyielding lumps when dry. I resolved never to touch the stuff again.

'Why don't you come along to clay modelling? It's fun.'

My friend's first suggestion of a retirement hobby is firmly squashed on the head. I recoil visibly. I mean, if your raffia mat's a flop you can always burn it, but what do you do with a failed pot? Put it in the fire and its deformity is preserved forever.

I managed, for the next 56 years to avoid clay. Then I visited our younger daughter. My grandson sidled up to me:

'Grandma, can you help me with my bowl?'

(Oh no – it's clay)

'It's messy' he says.

I sympathise, but cannot bear the thought of his lop-sided bowl being held up by the Miss Taylor of Jonathan's Infants' School in his first term. I weaken and borrow my daughter's yellow rubber gloves and get stuck in.

Clay in my grandson's hands!

From St. Nicholas Infants' school I progressed to St. Mary's Girls' Junior school, in an old building, with all female staff. All of them were single, for, if you married you were expected to leave. Arithmetic and English were our staple diet, and a high priority was put on spelling.

My parents were born in the 1890s and spelling had been important in their schools, as was the ability to learn every county town and the river across which it straddled. So I inherited the ability to chant, 'Lancashire, Lancaster on the Lune, and Yorkshire, York on the Ouse (and the Foss!)'. I also had spelling tests on birds, rivers, and flowers. For some reason my father instilled into me the spelling of PHLEGM (not a word I have often had cause to write!) and MISSISSIPPI. I can't think I have ever needed to know this, either. My father's prize bloom, both gardening and spelling-wise was CHRYSANTHEMUM. This word I learned to spell when I was eight. I wished I hadn't.

One day the pièce de résistance of St. Mary's Girls' school spelling test was CHRYSANTHEMUM. Miss Johnson was surprised when I spelt it correctly. Unfortunately the top class girls had stumbled at spelling MARIGOLD, and they held out no hope of tackling CHRYSANTHEMUM. To my everlasting embarrassment, at the tender age of eight, I was taken across the playground to the top class, and then paraded in front of them, to humiliate them with my correct spelling of that flower. No wonder they hated me.

What was worse was then being put up into Miss Smith's class, with the 'scholarship girls' when I was only nine. 'Clever Dick' was what they called me to begin with, but I soon found out that by whispering correct answers to my classmates, behind cupped hands held in front of my mouth, I curried favour, and became reasonably happy. Every morning started with the calling of the register, followed by Religious instruction, for this was a church school. In five mornings we encompassed Old Testament, New Testament, Prayer book, Catechism and a radio broadcast for schools. I have only to hear the first snatches of *Air on a G string* to be transported to that upstairs classroom where we sat listening to the schools' religious broadcast, our hands interlocked on top of our double wooden desks, with their inkwells full of scabby dried ink.

Physical education took place in a hard asphalt playground, where we did high jump over ever-heightening canes, with no landing mat. It was a good job we had a first-aider on the staff. Health and safety and risk assessment were unheard-of terms in those days! Handicraft lessons happened on two afternoons a week, and knitting played a prominent part, unless you were in the top class when you did sewing. My heart rejoiced at the fact that clay and raffia were not in the curriculum, but knitting most certainly was. My pink wool vest grew apace, and I duly did the cast off for the square neck. Progress down the back was boringly slow, so I pulled the side seam very taut, as I matched it with the front side seam, in order to receive the teacher's go ahead to sew it up. Having paid two shillings for my pink vest, I was expected to wear it. It was never a success. It itched incessantly, shrank in the wash, and never ever warmed my back, owing to my economy down the back straight.

After the pink vest knitting I progressed to knitting on four needles – firstly a useless little thimble bag, and then onto socks. Or should I say sock. We were put with a partner to choose what colour our joint pair would be - green with a rust stripe, or rust with a green stripe. We decided on the former. My partner was Sheila Short, who was taller than me but had dainty feet. Mine were large. The resultant joint pair of socks could inevitably belong to only one of us. We tossed. I won. One foot had plenty of wiggle-room; Sheila Short's tightly knitted green and rust creation applied a tourniquet to the other. This sock, together with later years of wearing stiletto heels, undoubtedly contributed to the formation of a troublesome bunion on my left foot!

However, despite a cold back and a numb foot I did survive the cold northeasterly winter winds by virtue of wearing a liberty bodice – a cream, striped vest-like garment with a woolly inside. The rubber suspenders dangling from the bottom were cut off, as I wore socks. At high school the wearing of a liberty bodice was a deep embarrassment; it meant that your parents were old and not enlightened enough to let you wear a bra. Some girls didn't even wear a vest! They would parade their coral pink 30A bras in front of us 'Cherub-vested' girls, and talk mystifyingly about 'not being able to go swimming today, because it's my *'off day'*. Sometimes they said they couldn't swim because they were *'on'*. I was switched neither off nor on so I swam every week, concealing my liberty bodice under a towel as I got changed into my turquoise 'cossie' made of bubbly nylon air pockets. Then I had to pull on my rubber flower-embossed hat, an agonising procedure which tugged my hair into its watertight enclosure. It also turned the shouts in the pool into muffled echoes, above which the swimming teacher boomed out, 'Forward, round together.'

She was called Miss Capstick, but we called her Catspit, and we were terrified of her. I gained my red badge for swimming a length but was glad to leave her classes before Catspit pushed me in from a crouched position, as a preliminary to diving. I did not want to be on the receiving end of artificial respiration.

Scared and scarred by my junior school experiences it is no surprise that I never learned to dive, have never worn green socks, and I have never ever liked chrysanthemums!

Chapter Three

Frisky the cat was a bit too frisky and met his death as he dashed heedlessly across the busy road outside our shop. He was laid to rest next to Sandy, in the salty garden plot, on which I placed a jam jar of flowers and a cross made from two twigs. The period of mourning was short, as soon on the scene came a pathetic kitten with a weeping eye. He appeared to be in a perpetual state of winking, so we called him Twink. He came from the farm of father's second cousin twice removed, in a village near Bridlington.

The day we went to collect Twink was the day I discovered how babies were born. The hot sun of that wonderful 1947 summer beat down on the farmyard, and despite the smell of muck I would rather have stayed outside. Instead I had to go into the overpoweringly warm kitchen with its all-the-year-round fire, on which sat precariously a sooty kettle spitting its boiling tea water over the coals. The grown ups were talking, as grown ups do. I sat on a speckled rag rug listening to the conversation.

On this particular day they weren't talking about the 'Big C' or funerals or anything interesting, so I slipped out into the farmyard. There was a terrific racket on the far side; a loud squawking and squeaking was coming from the pigsty. I managed to wedge the rounded end of my brown Clark's sandal between the slats and hoisted myself up to have a look.

There was this fat pig lying down snorting and puffing, its hairy pink belly going into ripples. Then out of its bottom slid a baby pig – all hot and steaming. I watched, entranced, as the big pig turned its head to investigate. For one horrid moment I thought she was going to eat it, but she just licked it and in a few moments another little pig came out, then another and another. I waited until 12 had come, then wrenched my sandal out of the slats and ran inside to tell my mum and dad how pigs were born. 'Come and see', I ordered. They looked at each other and laughed. I didn't realise then that they already knew. As we all crossed the cobbles the mother pig gave a loud squeal. Number 13 had made a late appearance.

Suddenly my dad let go of my hand and walked very quickly back to the house. Why didn't he want to look at the piglets?

The memory of that day on which the mystery of life and birth had been revealed has stayed imprinted in my memory. But the question remained – why had Dad rushed off when the pig squealed?

Six decades later, when war broke out in Iraq, I reached for the atlas so that I could get all the Middle Eastern countries into context. Iraq, with its great rivers of Tigris and Euphrates, had been the Garden of Eden. Mesopotamia was the land between two waters. Of course, that's where my dad had fought in the First World War. I went to the bookcase and took down the bulging green Family History book, in which are recorded our cars, our pets, our holidays and school prizes. In the Military section I found the pencilled account of my dad's time in 'Mess Pot'. I'd never studied it in detail before. But now the words Basra and Baghdad jumped before my eyes. He'd walked in this region in the searing desert sun, with little water and had eaten no food for three days.

I turned over the thin lined paper and saw he had scrawled on the back in thick pencil 'March 1917. Killed a man. He squealed like a pig.'

The mystery of the farmyard had been solved!

★★★★★★★★★★★★★★★★

Father's memories of the First World War were very real. He rarely told us of the grim side of life in the muddy trenches in France, though I do know that he had seen many of his colleagues gunned down. Instead he talked of the lighter side of those wartime years. Undoubtedly it had been his sense of humour that had kept up his spirits and those around him. He taught me to count in Hindustani, and regaled me with nonsense songs they had sung when trekking across the desert in Mesopotamia. One began 'Queen Mary, Queen Mary, please send me some socks, for we'll souvenir them when we're on the rocks...' I would listen, entranced, as he sang away sitting cross-legged on his tailor's table, hemming trousers. I loved to watch him chalk round patterns, and then hear the crisp cut of the shears. He rarely used pins; tailors baste rather than pin. Machining was done on a Singer treadle, which he had bought when he came out of the army and which now resides on the landing of our cottage in Wales, occasionally earning its keep when I make up new curtains.

When father made jackets he put interlining into the lapels, and to make the canvas lie flat he would machine criss-cross patterns. Sometimes he would deftly twist and turn the cloth and embroider my name. I wonder how many men have unknowingly carried 'Margaret Jefferson' across their chests?

Buttonholing was a skilled job. This needed strong thread, which I was allowed to pull across a cone of bees wax to stop it knotting. Another of my jobs was to supply father with a steady stream of wet cloths for the pressing operation – done with very heavy irons, heated on a precarious gas ring in the corner of the shop. In this corner there was a mysterious pile of soft, cream packets. Ladies who came in and asked for 'S.Ts' were given one of these packets, and for some reason, which I never fathomed, father tore off the paper sleeve label, and the ladies hid their purchase at the bottom of their shopping baskets.

Curiosity got the better of me, and one day I dared to undo a packet and I drew out an oblong pad of cotton wool with loops at each end, and I secreted it in my bedroom. I am sorry now for the lady who bought that packet. She was short-changed. She had nine pads. The tenth was already in use in my bedroom, and I must say it made an excellent little hammock for my smallest doll!

Between the front room, which was the shop, and our living room, was a little window so that we could see when customers came in. This also meant that customers could peer into our room, although their view was partly obliterated by Beethoven.

A mock marble statuette of mother's favourite composer stood proudly on top of the piano. We rarely saw his face, as Beethoven was the repository for mother's best hat, which she wore for church, for Bible Society, Mothers' Union and Townswomen's Guild meetings. One day when she was out and my father was in the back yard I heard an insistent tapping on the shop counter. Climbing onto the piano stool I could see a lady in an overall waiting to be served. I decided to try my hand at being a shopkeeper so went through to the shop and asked her what she wanted.

'Has your dad any nylons?' she asked.

I knew he had, and I knew where he kept them.

'Oh yes,' I answered proudly, ' they're under the counter.'

With that she rushed out of the shop and called to a waiting gaggle of factory girls from the local ropery, 'Come on girls – Mr Jefferson's got nylons.'

Of course these 'under the counter nylons' were for his best customers only. I didn't understand such strategies and I can remember feeling aggrieved that my father hadn't showered me with gratitude for filling his shop with such eager customers. No longer would the ropery girls have to dye their legs with gravy browning, and draw lines down the back with brown crayons to emulate the seams.

The shop counter was made of very solid wood. Barry, my brother used to sleep inside it during the war, as a protection from bombs. My cot was put under the piano, for the same reason, though sometimes during an air raid I was taken with my sister Beryl and my mother into the tiny cupboard under the stairs. I can still recall the clicking of the electricity meter and the stale smell of gas, and, over sixty years later, I hate being cooped up in a cramped space. I also hate the sound of aeroplanes droning, and in war museums, when they sound the siren I feel quivers running down my back.

The 'All Clear siren' was a welcome sound, but it came with a cost. Father was treasurer at St. Nicholas church in Beverley, and hit on the brilliant idea of raising money. The local printers made sturdy blue cardboard collecting boxes which were distributed to the parishioners with the injunction that every time the All Clear siren sounded they should put in a threepenny bit or some pennies in thankfulness that they were still alive. Over a hundred boxes came over to our house twice a year for the counting ceremony. I loved making piles of 12 pennies, 4 threepenny bits or 2 sixpences, and then regimenting them into 20 columns to make up a pound. 'Jeff's boxes', as they came to be known, kept the church finances in the black throughout the war. When it ended my father did not let the donors off the hook. 'Put something in every week in thankfulness that we are at peace' he told them. And they did!

★★★★★★★★★★★★★★★

I never had pocket money, but I did have chocolate. Inside the shop counter was a shelf on which lay a bar of chocolate from which I was allowed one piece when I came in from school. Considering the stringent rationing I think I must have consumed more than my fair share. There was blended chocolate, with its delightful mix of plain and milk chocolate, the ever popular Kit Kat, and the special treat of Caley's Tray, in a cream wrapper bearing the pictures of the six large filled chocolates, all joined together. Mother had the Turkish delight and I had the caramel because neither mother nor father could eat that comfortably with their false teeth!

When I recount my wartime chocolate memories to my husband, I am amazed to hear that he was very spoiled on the chocolate front. Michael's father's parishioners pooled their coupons in order to provide chocolate for the vicar's son, who was evacuated away from the bombs of Birmingham, and later Sunderland.

Michael was born in August, but as he was a tiny premature baby he was still in Loveday Street hospital in Birmingham when war was declared on September 3rd. With his mother he was then evacuated to the Clee Hills, and subsequently to Bourton-on-the-Hill in the Cotswolds, where his mother shared a house with another clergy wife with the same name – Mrs Walker. Her baby was called Margaret, and she and Michael were put out in adjacent prams. I can now tease him and say that he has slept with a Margaret Walker for most of his life!

Later in the war, when his father moved to a parish near Sunderland, Michael moved to Barnard Castle to stay with his mother's family. They too made sure he had plenty to eat, and, according to the detailed diary, written by his mother during their evacuation, he was even given a banana! Even now I am filled with envy.

Bananas and oranges were the forbidden fruits of my childhood – forbidden only because of their scarcity. Then one day the news arrived: 'Rutherford's shop has oranges and bananas in'. My mother placed me in the fruit queue and went off to queue for fish. I could see beautiful round orange balls – they looked good, and certainly better than those crooked yellow things which looked bruised and mottled. I stood on tiptoe as I neared the counter, only to see the last two oranges go into a lady's basket. Tears dropped slowly down my infant cheek, but the green-grocer said 'never mind, love, have two bananas instead.'

My older brother and sister had told me how nice they were, and I couldn't wait to try one. I bit well into its side, tried chewing it, then spat it out in disgust and howled. Bananas were not nice; they were horrid and bitter. No one had told me that you had to peel them first!

Chapter Four

One thing our family never stinted on during the war was milk. Our various cats appreciated this, and soon learned that the back doorstep was the place to be in the early morning. We had not just one milkman, but two! First came Mr Robinson with his pony and cart. He would come through our back gate, across the tiny yard to the doorstep, which mother had brightened to a violent orange with her donkey stone. There he would read the card under the big white jug and go back to his cart to measure out in his quart and pint metal jugs the amount required, pour it out into our jug and replace the saucer on top. This would be hastily brought into the pantry, and another jug put out before the arrival of Mr Harrison, milkman number two, with his pony and trap. I never thought it odd that we had two milkmen and assumed everyone did. In fact it was a tactical issue: Mr Robinson was a good customer in our shop, so deserved our custom on the milk scene. Mr Harrison had a teenage daughter, Shirley, who helped my mother with the infants' classes in the Sunday school. Mother was keen that this family had a share of our largesse in the milk quota.

To stop the milk curdling in the heat or freezing in the ice it was put on the slab in our pantry, the jugs being veiled with net covers from which hung little beads to weigh them down. These were fly prevention tactics. Meat, butter and cheese were put under the slab in the meat safe, whose door was a wire mesh with a little latch. Bread loaves were stored in an earthenware crock on a stool, under which stood the bucket of 'put-down' eggs. Flour came in cloth bags, and sugar in blue paper bags with cleverly folded tops.

Hair washing took place in the scullery once a week. Mother collected rainwater in an evil-smelling vat in the backyard, as this would lather up better than the tap water, which, in a limestone area, was very hard. Before the era of shampoo I used to help grate washing soap into green slivers. Jugs of hot water were poured over my head, and the slivers of soap applied – though I can't remember them ever making much of a lather. Powdered Vaseline shampoo with its lovely fragrance was a major improvement. Vinegar was put into the rinsing water, and my hair was rough-towelled dry before I knelt down on the hearthrug to dry it off by the fire. If there was a party in the offing I had to go through the misery of rags being twisted round half-dry hair. They were agony to put in and agony to sleep on, and by the time the party started my fine hair was already as straight as a die. The alternative, but similarly futile way to make my hair curl, was to be sent across the road to Mrs Tomlinson who attacked it with tongs heated up in her fire. They came perilously close to my scalp and the stench of scorched hair was horrendous. I resolved to grow my hair and opt for plaits or bunches tied up with pretty ribbons rather than have a perpetually branded scalp.

Apart from the small stone sink in the scullery the only other furniture was a grey and white gas stove, a chest of drawers to hold dusters, cleaning materials and my mother's piano music, a very small table on which were done the cooking and the ironing, and the boiler into which mother plunged sheets, pillowcases, hankies and dad's shirts every Monday morning. The other washing equipment – the tin bath, washboard, dolly tub, dolly stick and posser - lived in the outside shed with the bikes. Twisting the dolly stick was probably very good for the waistline, but it was very tiring. Possing was much more fun. Lifting the long wooden handle with a perforated copper dome on the bottom and then squelching it down into the tub of *Rinso-ed* or *Oxydol-ed* washing resulted in a slurp-gurgle sound that was intensely satisfying. Washday lasted most of Monday by the time clothes had been scrubbed, boiled, Reckitt's blued, hand-rinsed, starched and put through the mangle. Monday lunches were served in a billow of steam, and were usually cold minced up bits of Sunday's meat, moistened with gravy and served with a jacket potato. Sometimes, however, if it was a fine day and the washing was going well, mother would cook my favourite – egg and chips to which I added more salt than I now know was healthy, and a generous pouring of brown vinegar.

The backyard was so tiny that we had a double washing line, with a huge clothes prop, which paraded father's long johns and mother's voluminous, interlock bloomers above the wooden railings for the whole of Denton Street to see. I had to help my mother tweak the sheets into a good shape before they were hung onto the line. I held onto the corners for dear life after once having the sheet tugged out of my little hand, only to drop onto the grit of the back yard, and thus needing a re-wash. There were no clip pegs in those days, so our clothes were at the mercy of wooden ones made by the gypsies.

Because we had a shop in what would have been our front room, we had only one other room besides the scullery. It was small, had no right -angles, and included a cubbyhole under the stairs where we hung our coats. Father was no good at painting or carpentry or mending broken electrical items, but he was good at papering and laying lino, as, being a tailor, he was well used to measuring accurately and cutting patterns. So our floor-covering was lino, helped out with rag rugs, which my mother, my sister and I 'pegged' by pushing strips of old suits and dresses into a sack backing. My grandchildren come back from school visits to tell of 'how they made rugs in the olden days' and hopefully think they are telling me something new!

We had a lot of furniture in a small room – large sideboard, gate-legged table, dining chairs, a small leatherette settee and one armchair, a piano and a china cabinet on top of a cupboard. This was my parents' second marriage, after both had been widowed. Father's first wife, Blanche, had died of cancer in her thirties, and mother's first husband, Walter, had died of pneumonia leaving her with two small children. She had eked out a miniscule widow's pension by giving piano lessons from her home in Pype Hayes, Birmingham. She was also a churchgoer, leader of the Girls' Life Brigade, and a church magazine distributor. It was while she was collecting the annual subscription for the magazine that she was invited into the house where by chance a widower from Beverley was staying with his deceased wife's sister. It was a real Mills and Boon romance, culminating in marriage in 1938 and my arrival in 1940. Squeezing a family of five into the back room of a corner shop, with only two bedrooms was a challenge. My brother had to sleep in a camp bed in the bathroom, which I thought was normal. I remember being surprised on going into other people's bathrooms and not finding any bed there.

Crockery was put in the large wall cupboard of our living room. Under it was the cutlery drawer and to the right of it a mixture of items unknown to the present generation – silk for mending stockings, darning mushrooms, and 'peggers' for making rag rugs. On the top shelf, in a place I could not possibly reach, even if I stood on the settee, was the resting place for flower vases, trifle bowls and presents that were not meant to be seen until my birthday, or Christmas. On one occasion my parents put on the top shelf a Christmas present, which I had already played with, but which was out of bounds until I could be trusted to control my emotions! It was a circular puzzle in which the aim was to get three little ball bearings to go round a maze and end up in the middle. I think it was made by Chad Valley and can clearly remember the pink pigs on a blue background. I can also remember getting extremely frustrated at not being able to do this aggravating puzzle. I cried in sheer desperation. My father did not believe in people crying. Even if I hurt myself I was told 'Be brave, Margaret – be a brave girl'. To cry in frustration was not tolerated either. The offending puzzle was put on the top shelf for three months. Nowadays, when tempted to scream at a locked up computer I mentally 'put it on the top shelf' and walk away and do something else until I can trust myself to deal with the situation more calmly!

In the other corner of the room stood the china cabinet with a leaded glass front behind which was arranged my grandparents' wedding present tea service, which was never used, as the cups were so wide that the tea became cold too quickly. In front of this was a silver teapot - the repository for all things valuable – including father's spare false teeth, and a ten-shilling note, for emergency use only. Pound notes were riches indeed, and on the rare occasions my father was given a five-pound note in the shop he would bring it for me to look at. I remember it as being large, white and with black feathery ornate writing. Under the cabinet stood a mahogany cupboard, which held a range of exotic treasures, among which were an ivory fan, a feather fan, an ebony elephant and an ostrich egg. This was the place where the artificial Christmas tree was kept. It was not an impressive specimen – only about 16 inches high, with pathetic arms that bent out, and which had lost much of their greenery. At the end of each arm was a metal holder, supposedly for a tiny candle, but we never used these. It didn't take much decorating – one twist of tinsel, a few paper decorations and a star, and it was done. I wasn't an envious child, by and large, although I did cast a wandering eye over my friend Pamela's red tap shoes, and yes, I was jealous when I saw her big 'proper' Christmas tree with shiny baubles.

Help was at hand. My brother Barry, eleven years older than me, cycled several miles along East Yorkshire country roads until he came to a wood, where he hacked down an adolescent fir tree, and somehow managed to drag it back home. Instead of compliments ringing in his ears at his kindness in cheering up his young sister, he received a good thrashing from my father who would not tolerate any form of stealing. However, as the tree could not be restored or replanted, it was allowed to stay. The china cabinet and cupboard were moved upstairs to make way for the huge fir, which was stuck into the washtub. Its top hit the ceiling and had to be bent, as if in humiliation for being stolen property. Mother and I made paper chains and lanterns to brighten it up, and I could not wait until Boxing Day when my friend Pamela would see it.

It was a Christmas to remember. Not only did I have my one and only real tree, but I also had a wriggly snake, made by Uncle Alf from pieces of painted wood stuck onto a tape, with a plucked piece of feather for the fang. This was even better than the Rupert Annual, which was a yearly treat in my pillowcase on Christmas morning, along with the apple, orange and sixpence, and the rather disappointing parcels of hankies and socks from well meaning aunts. The other memorable present was a new doll made from red felt and with a celluloid face. I named her Belinda, and she was second only to Christine, my favourite doll who had a pot head.

Belinda was not mine for long. The young daughter of a Townswomen's Guild friend of my mother was rushed into hospital with meningitis. As she was the same age as me it was considered 'a good thing' if I were to send Belinda to the hospital as a present. I agreed readily, as I was sure that Belinda was only on a temporary visit and would be returned when the little girl recovered. Not so. The girl was in an isolation ward, and after she had died nothing was returned. I imagine Belinda was cremated.

I was near to tears, but father's 'be brave, Margaret' rang in my juvenile ears.

I know that my father meant well and for the most part I am grateful for his maxims, which he chanted frequently and which became part of our family's mantra:

'Never put off till tomorrow, what you can do today'.

'A stitch in time saves nine'.

'Never trouble trouble till trouble troubles you'.

'If a job's worth doing, it's worth doing well'

'Pride goes before a fall'.

Over that one memorable childhood Christmas of my fiendish puzzle, my illicit Christmas tree and my beloved Belinda I had learned that crying from frustration is non-productive, that stealing is evil, even if it is done from genuinely altruistic motives, and that helping others involves sacrifice.

I had also learned that having a good cry, for whatever reason, ultimately made me feel better, but that it was better to put on a smile for father, and to let the deluge of tears wait until I was safely under the blankets.

Chapter Five

Wartime or not, we still had holidays. Father's shop was shut for the first week of August, when the local shipyard and rope works had their annual break. During the war we used to go to Hornsea; it was only 13 miles away, but it was a thrill to go on the bus and to stay in someone else's house, though I believe I succeeded in locking myself in the lavatory on my very first holiday. I can't remember this, though I do have very clear memories of being taken to Hornsea by my mother in a bid to cure my whooping cough.

Whooping cough was viewed quite seriously. After a month of whooping I was taken to every set of road works mother could find. I was told to stand near the tar pile and breathe in deeply. The cough persisted and when we could find no more East Riding roads in need of repairing, a special trip to Hornsea was planned. Cocooned in scarf, glove and pixie hat I was marched to the sea front, which was still screened with barbed wire and concrete blocks, and commanded to inhale the January sea air. The tide was in, and I was denied the pleasure of a beach walk. I was cold, miserable, still whooping and now I was crying.

'Mummy – why is the beach closed today? Can we come tomorrow – and will it be open then?'

Measles and German measles are only vague memories, but I clearly remember having chicken pox. Although the itching was unpleasant, I quite enjoyed my enforced bed rest, and being allowed to sleep on a camp bed in my parents' room, away from my sister and brother. Days were long and peaceful, with little naps punctuated by colouring books and puzzles. It was winter, so mother carried a shovel full of smouldering coals from the downstairs room to put in the tiny black-leaded bedroom grate. In those days the Doctor actually came to the house and made you feel really important. He also prescribed delicious cherry medicine as 'a tonic'. Psychological, no doubt, but it worked! Malt was given in a further attempt to 'build me up' and calamine lotion was liberally smeared on the spots. I was told not to scratch the tops off; the existing scar on my right calf is testimony to my failure to comply.

After the war, when my measling, whooping and scratching had ended, we went to a Bed and Breakfast establishment in Bridlington for our holidays. The terraced guesthouse at number 41 was run by a lady called Kathleen and her mother. I think they must have slept in the kitchen, as they took in three families, who had to share one bathroom and one lavatory. Rules were strict: you could have one bath a week if you booked in advance and paid extra; you had to be out of the house from 10 a.m. until 5 p.m. and sand had to be tipped out of your sandals before crossing the threshold.

The family at the next table 'spoke funny'. Their name was odd too – Blenkinsopp. They were from Lancashire and had a six-year-old son called Micky. I was terrified of his parents after hearing screams from Micky on the second evening, followed by a loud slamming of the door, and then muffled sobbing. What on earth had they done to the poor boy? The next morning Micky gave me a toothless grin over the breakfast table. His mother had tied cotton tightly round his wobbly front tooth and attached the other end of the cotton to the doorknob, and then slammed the door. I spent that morning frantically wiggling my own loose tooth and twisting it round and round on its stalk of skin, eventually succeeding in pulling it out before Mrs Blenkinsopp could get her beady eyes on it.

Micky found my parents less officious than his own, so came on the beach with us, doing delightful things like burying me in sand, wielding a wooden spade over me and singing:
'Margaret Jefferson is no good.
Chop her up for firewood.
When she is dead, stand her on her head.
Then we shall all eat currant bread.'

In return I would sing:
'Micky Blenkinsopp is a funny one
with a nose like a pickled onion.
His face is a squashed tomato.
His legs are drumsticks.'

I also retaliated by deliberately mispronouncing his surname and calling him Micky Blinking Slop. I wonder if he is still alive, and if he married and had children. If so I hope that Mrs Blenkinsopp the Second never attached cotton to her children's milk teeth.

The compensation for the long, cold winter of 1947 was a gloriously hot summer. Father's shop had done well that year as soldiers who had been 'demobbed' had to buy new trousers. This was the only time we had two weeks' holiday, a week at Kathleen's in Bridlington, and a week in a B & B near Peasholm Park in Scarborough. Every day we cooled ourselves down in the outdoor swimming pool by the North Bay. Mother held me up by the straps of my stretchy knitted swimming costume while I thrashed my legs around and tried to do breast stroke. By the end of the week I could swim. I also had to put my head under water – which I hated – as mother went down the water slide and laughed so much that her false teeth flew out, and I had to retrieve them from the bottom of the pool. The swimming session always ended with a hot drink from the pool café. Father had Bovril, but I always had Horlicks in a thick large mug with a silly handle that was all filled in and had no place for your fingers.

Mother was not keen on seaside amusement arcades, but my father used to take me in, if the weather was wet, and arm me with a load of pennies. Sometimes I would have a run of good luck, when the metal balls I flicked up in the machine would fall into the right hole, and I would get a penny back and be able to have another go. Of course the arcade always won the money back, but not before I had done the rounds of the other machines. I could never resist one where a jointed metal hand could be lowered and then made to grasp its fingers around the chosen object. Joy of joys when it actually scooped up the object. Sorrow of sorrows when I carefully raised the hand and swung it to the hole where it should have dropped my prize, only to see it slither out of the metal fingers at the last moment. There was a tall booth where a crane was manoeuvred in a similar way, but with strings that let down the scoop. I had never seen people have success in lifting up their chosen bit of jewellery or toy, but this did not deter me from having my annual go.

Father would then guide me past the row of machines where grown men were chortling. I was left wondering what was so enthralling about 'what the butler saw' as I was steered to the row of gaily-painted clowns who swung their smiley faces to and fro – their mouths open, awaiting the ping pong ball which they regurgitated through their pipe throats into numbered channels, though usually into low numbered ones, which did not qualify for a prize. One day, however, I succeeded - but where was father? He had missed my brilliant ball throwing. I soon found him, as I could already hear him laughing hysterically. He could never resist putting a penny into the Laughing Policeman machine. 'Ha, ha, ha, ha; hee, hee, hee; ho, ho, ho…' Soon everyone around was laughing uncontrollably, and we left the arcade feeling our pennies and halfpennies had been well spent, even though we had only aching cheek muscles and my prize of a plastic toy to show for our expenditure.

We travelled to the seaside by train, which was a thrill, although I think I was more excited by the journey to Beverley Railway station in a taxi. The driver loaded our cases and let down a folding seat so that I could sit facing my parents. We never had a car, so this journey in a motor vehicle was an annual treat, as was lunch on the following day. This was the day that we ate in 'The Golden Egg' café, which put on a three-course lunch for 3/9d. The tables had real cloths and very heavy cutlery and condiment sets. The waitresses were dressed in black with frilly white aprons, and when they came to take our order I knew it would always be the same: tomato soup, roast beef and Yorkshire pudding with carrots and tinned peas, followed by apple pie and custard. I didn't like peas then, but forced myself to eat them, knowing that father had forked out hard earned money for this family treat – a meal which mother didn't have to cook and after which we didn't have to do the washing up!

And where was our cat while we were living it up at the seaside? I don't think there were such places as catteries in those days. Neighbours were called in to feed Twink. Our neighbours were called the Bicks. Mr Bick was a Russian and I think his name was really Bickov, but they knocked the 'ov 'off. Their youngest son, Alfie, was in his twenties and was frightened of the wireless, as he thought green men were going to come out of it and take him away. He liked music, so they bought him a harmonium, which was put in his bedroom, whose wall was a shared one with our bathroom. Sometimes he played tunes, but when the moon was full he degenerated into playing scales – up and down, up and down, for two hours at a time. Once I tried banging on the wall to shut him up, but that sent him off into a rage with a torrent of swear words that were worse than the scales. I used to worry about what he would do to our cat, but mother said stroking the cat was good for him. In any case Alfie soon disappeared from the scene and went to live in a special hospital outside the town. He had schizophrenia, which sounded worse than either constipation or whooping cough, so I was glad that he had gone, as I certainly didn't want to catch it.

Between the Bicks' back yard and ours was a coalhouse, where we used to hang our house key when we went out, and a bicycle shed where I loved to play shops and hospitals. Children from the back street crammed into its dark creosoted interior awaiting my diagnosis, and retreating before I could perform surgery on them with bicycle spanners or enemas with bicycle pumps!

Between the bike shed and the coalhouse was our lavatory. The wooden door didn't fit, and had a convenient six-inch gap at the top, through which we aimed tennis balls. Five points if you got it through the gap, but ten points if you got it into the lavatory pan. Mind you, you deserved ten points, as you had to plunge your hands into the icy water to retrieve the squidgy ball. In winter we replaced the tennis balls with snowballs. It was a pity my father was in residence when I took my winning shot. He leapt out of the lavatory, trousers round his knees and walloped me very hard. Nowadays Health and Safety acts would probably prohibit outside lavatories, and my father would be worrying about Child Protection laws.

You certainly needed a risk assessment before going to our lavatory. In winter it was inadvisable to sit on the seat. Tearing the skin of your bottom from a frozen seat was painful, bearing in mind that it had later to be wiped with either newspaper, or later by the afore-mentioned Izal Medicated toilet roll. Whoever invented soft tissue toilet rolls deserves an O.B.E.

You also had to mind your head as mother always draped seaweed from the chain mechanism. Visitors who ventured there unknowingly at night were known to cry out in alarm as they reached up to flush, and found strands of serrated bladderwrack entwining rubbery fingers around their arms.

I always liked bladderwrack – not only for its apt name for a toilet location, but also because I loved pressing the little bladders and hearing them pop. This seaweed wasn't just decorous, but functional too. When it was crisp and dry it presaged an anticyclone and good weather. When it was limp and wet then rain was imminent. A rough and ready form of meteorological prediction, but possibly more reliable than a certain modern day weather forecaster!

That salty, healthy smell which obscured other lavatorial odours still evokes memories of summer holidays in Bridlington: bathing huts, striped canvas deck chairs, metal buckets, wooden spades, penny slot machines, thermos flasks, Smith's crisp with little blue twists holding the salt, greaseproof packets of egg sandwiches, and the treat of a threepenny cornet and a bottle of sarsaparilla.

The 1940s were ending. Gradually things were returning to normal, although sweets were still rationed. My time at junior school was ending, and the spectre of 'The County Exam – the Eleven Plus' was looming. A brand new Secondary Modern school was being built, and I really wanted to go there rather than 'pass my scholarship' and have to go to Beverley Girls' High School. This was for posh children who lived at the top end of the town, and not for children like us who played under the streetlight in the back street.

There were seasons for balls, for whips and tops, for conkers, fives, marbles, hopscotch and skipping. We skipped forwards and backwards, with folded arms and with double spins of the rope, called 'bumps'. We ran into the big turning rope with chants of

'All in together girls,
never mind the weather girls,
by I count two
you've got to touch your shoe.
One – two' (then you had to touch your shoe and keep on skipping,
ready for:
'by I count four you've got to touch the floor' and later 'by I count
six, you've got to do the splits'.)

We played 'Queenie', and a game in which you progressed to the far wall by taking a stride if the letter of the alphabet called out was in your name. This was one of the few occasions when I have thanked my parents for christening me Dorothy Margaret Jefferson. I nearly always won this game!

The other pastime in which I excelled was doing handstands. I had perfected headstands by the time I was four, when I embarrassed my parents, let alone the vicar and congregation at the parish garden fête. As churchwarden's daughter I was chosen to present the bouquet to the Mayoress who opened the event. After thrusting the chrysanthemums (yes, I can still spell it!) into her hands I proceeded to stand on my head on the vicarage lawn. My new blue long frilly dress fell down to reveal a pair of waving legs and a pair of navy knickers. 'But they're clean' I protested when my parents indicated their displeasure!

Hide and Seek was a favourite game, which went under a variety of names according to which part of the country you hailed from. I have heard it called Relievo, and Lievo 123 and in the West Riding there was a strange rule by which you could make yourself immune from being caught by calling out something that sounded like 'keast'. In Beverley you had to run to the post and shout 'Bricky, one, two, three.' I can't remember what these magic words did. Maybe I never got to the post quickly enough!

I do remember the different ways we had of choosing who was to be 'on' for a game. There was 'Eenie-meanie-miney-mo, whose subsequent words are now classed as racist, and 'One potato, two potato, three potato, four…' But the way I liked best was the revolting practice of spitting on all four fingers and thumb, rubbing them into the dust in the gutter, and then seeing which finger had the most dirt on. With five children standing in front of you it was then easy to correlate children and fingers, and determine who would be the chaser, or who would hide first.

Obviously a girl who subscribed to such dirty practices was not a suitable candidate for Beverley Girls' High School, who aimed to turn out 'ladies'. I didn't want to become posh, so I decided that I would rather go to the brand new Secondary Modern school. This was incomprehensible to my family who had never had anyone at a grammar school.

Unfortunately, unlike most of my back street playmates, I passed my scholarship. Time to wash my dirty fingers and put away childish things…

Chapter Six

'Don't stay for school dinners' was the advice I was given before going to the high school.

'You have to eat frog spawn and sometimes fly pudding.'

I gathered later that these were the names for sago pudding and spotted dick.

'Mrs Mackenzie stands behind you until you've eaten up all your cabbage.'

I resolved not to be subjected to frogspawn, fly pudding or Mrs Mackenzie. I would go home for dinner.

When I passed my scholarship I was allowed to draw out all my savings from the Yorkshire Penny Bank, into which I had dutifully paid 6d a week into my blue school bankbook since 1945. I bought a Hercules three-quarter-size bicycle on which to ride the mile to school and back twice a day.

Most days I was early for school, but there were two things which made me late: one was the level crossing gates being shut, often for shunting operations at Cherry Tree Lane. However this engendered an interest in locomotive numbers, which was to stand me in good stead with my future fiancé. The second thing was 'dogs', in particular a black Labrador who lay in wait for me to emerge into his street, and who would then race alongside, snapping at my heels. To avoid this dog I worked out innumerable alternative routes to school, and vowed never to have a dog, and certainly not a Labrador.

Post-war years in the early 1950s were exciting. First there was the Festival of Britain in 1951. The headmistress of Beverley High School, Miss Davies, refused permission for my parents to take me off school to join the church trip to London for the day. She did not believe that it would be 'educational'. I never questioned how my parents managed it, but to the Festival I went – to see the Skylon, and the Dome of Discovery, and to enjoy a river trip to the Battersea pleasure gardens with their magic mirrors and ghost trains. Here Dad and I got separated from Mother, and back at King's Cross station we had an anxious wait. A minute before the excursion train was due to leave, she arrived with three elderly ladies in tow. Being in a hurry, mother had tried to get them onto the underground, but Mrs Bick (the one who was really Mrs Bickov but who had knocked the 'ov' off) had panicked on seeing a staircase that moved, and had refused to get on the escalator. They had had to pool their remaining money to pay for a taxi.

Back at school I survived the first year well and began to be a bit glad that I had passed my scholarship. Never one to fuss about clothes I was quite pleased to have a uniform, which took away decision making on what to wear. On top of the afore-mentioned Cherub vest, liberty bodice and navy knickers, went a white blouse, navy pleated gymslip, striped blue and white tie and a navy V necked pullover.

The gymslip had to be three inches from the floor when you were kneeling – which you had to do for prayers at the morning assembly. It was stressed upon us that we must close our eyes tightly during the prayers and I wonder if the staff went around secretly with tape measures while we were praying, to check that our gymslips were neither too long nor too short! In the summer we wore candy-striped dresses in our house colours, with white Peter Pan collars. Berets were worn the whole year through, and you were not allowed to eat ice cream on the way home from school. Ice cream and school uniform did not mix!

One cold February morning in my second year (Lower IV) I was sitting at my desk by the window in the upstairs classroom in Norwood House – a fine Georgian house that was part of the school. Miss Robinson, the French mistress, a small and round little body, was taking us through the imperfect tense. I joined in the communal chanting, but happened to look out of the window just as a flag was being hoisted on the tower of Beverley Minster.

'Miss, Miss,' I interjected loudly in the middle of the French chant.

'Mademoiselle, s'il vous plait' replied Miss Robinson.

'Mademoiselle Robinson' I shouted, with the smug satisfaction of knowing something nobody else yet knew. *'Le roi est mort!'*

My news was greeted with ridicule, and I was told to sit down and stop being so silly.

I continued to gaze at the Minster towers, and I knew that the Union flag was flown at half-mast only for famous people.

Ten minutes later I was vindicated. There was a knock at the classroom door. A prefect whispered something to Miss Robinson, whose face went as white as the chalk she was holding. She sniffed into her hanky, wiped her eyes and with a tremor in her voice announced – in English – *'The King is dead. Long live the Queen.'* The close proximity of these two statements still surprises me. To a class of 11 and 12-year olds it was a signal for laughter. Miss Robinson was not impressed. Her subsequent announcement, that the class was dismissed and that we could all go home, was greeted with enthusiastic cheers. We had no television at home, but I remember the radio playing hours of solemn music, and of being cross that the king was to be buried on February 15th, my birthday, and that my party had to be postponed until March 15th.

There was another death during my schooldays. Our cat Twink snuffed it too. However our Latin teacher, Miss Barnes, had found a stray kitten and brought it to school so she could feed it during the day. She was delighted that I offered to adopt it. I wrapped it in my school scarf, held it close to my chest and walked home for lunch, accompanied by my friend Jill. Crossing the allotments we saw smoke coming out of the church roof, then flames. We ran home, alerted my dad who rushed over to Auntie Dora's to ring the fire brigade, then dropped the kitten in the scullery and ran back to the church. I had just done my fireman's badge at Guides, so stood by the fire hydrant ready to point it out to Beverley Fire Brigade, who, I am sure, didn't need my help! Meanwhile my mother was carrying out the worthy, though foolhardy task of ferrying out the new hymnbooks from the back of church, as smouldering bits of pine roof were falling around her.

Deprived of my moment of glory in bearing the news of the king's death, I was now able to rejoice in the acclamation in the newspaper and on the radio in 'News from the North' on the BBC Home Service – 'Schoolgirl's alarm and churchwarden's caution save Beverley church from fire.' At the next Guide parade in church, my friend Jill and I were each presented with a gold cross and chain, as a token of appreciation from the St. Nicholas congregation. Jill went on to become a Church Army officer, working in prisons; I was to marry a vicar. These crosses were worn often. And what about the stray kitten? Abandoned in the scullery where dinner was in the process of being served up – what else could he do but to scoff the lot? With the sound of spurting charred wood still ringing in our ears we didn't need to look any further for a name for this cat. He was christened 'Squib'.

Chapter Seven

S quib was still going strong when I left school to go to university in Nottingham. There, for the first time in my life, I was pet-less. The warden of my hall of residence, Miss Spelman, however, had a treat for all the students who were on 'telephone duty'. In pre-mobile phone days the public telephone near the entrance to the hall had to be 'manned' to take incoming calls for the students. Two were rostered each evening, so that one could run up stairs and around corridors to summon the student to the phone.

After our two hour stint of telephone duty Miss Spelman would arrive with 'Peter', an elderly King Charles spaniel on his lead. Dog lovers or not (and I was most certainly not) we had to take the unenthusiastic beast up the University drive until it had performed its duty. As Miss Spelman was also a lecturer in my department – Social Administration – it behoved me to keep on the right side of her. To give credit where it was due she was a good warden. Only once did I see her really lose her temper. She was a great one for putting up lists on her notice board. Woe betides us if we neglected to read her daily missives. One day one of her lists had been removed. She was furious, and put up a big notice on the board, demanding in capital letters, 'WHERE'S MY LIST?'

I give full credit to the unknown student who dared to pin up, in reply, another notice that said. '30 DEGREES TO STARBOARD'

It was to Miss Spelman that we had to make a personal request if we were to leave the Hall of Residence for even one night in term time. 'She who ruled Florence Boot Hall' was to be obeyed, and a dire fate awaited those caught entertaining gentlemen in their rooms without a chaperone! As for one of the girls in Hall who became pregnant – well, it was instant expulsion from university for her!

All my clothes, books and other necessities had to be packed into one trunk, to be sent in advance by British Rail or British Road Services at the beginning of the academic year, and my bike came with me on the train. These were the days before computers and the myriad of electric and electronic gadgets that are necessities for present-day students. I was impressed, however, by a Law student who had a clean towel every day, and whose grandmother paid the postage for the weekly laundering. Equally impressive was another student who had two pairs of clean knickers for every day of the week. Fifty years later I was in the vicinity of her home and phoned to see if I could call. 'Well, it's not really convenient' she replied,' you see it's my wash day'! (Maybe she gets through three pairs of knickers a day in her old age!)

My roommate, Barbara, was from Farnworth, near Bolton, and despite occasional rivalry between my White

Rose allegiance and her Red Rose, we got on very well. I still have the recipe for the delicious Ovaltine loaf, which her mother used to arm her with at the beginning of each term. Meals in hall were very good – cooked breakfasts, and cooked lunches every day, high tea on Wednesday and Saturday, afternoon tea on Sunday and formal dinners on all other days. For these it was required that you lined up in good time outside the dining hall, dressed in 'a dark and respectable frock', over which you wore your gown. You did not sit down until the grand procession had arrived at the High Table, which was replete with candelabra (purple candles on the occasion that Archbishop Michael Ramsay was a guest during Lent.)

Before the maids served up soup, the grace was sung in Latin by a select group of girls. The words were always the same: *'Benedictus benedicat, per Jesum Christum dominum nostrum. Amen.'* By accident I found myself in this 'Grace choir'. At the Freshers' conference I had been press-ganged into giving blood, and the girl on the next bed chatted to me. Gill was a music student, and on hearing that I could play the piano and violin, and enjoyed singing, she promptly earmarked me for future events.

In the December of our first term Gill was in the sick bay with tonsillitis. It was her week to compose the music for the Latin grace and she didn't feel up to doing it.

'You do it – Margaret' she implored. This showed a great amount of misplaced confidence in me as a composer. The grace was traditionally sung in two parts in the style of Palestrina. I had never even heard of him, let alone had an insight into his composition style. Come to think of it I had never even composed anything in the style of Margaret Jefferson, let alone Palestrina.

I had just pencilled in some stave lines and perfected my curly treble clef, when a message came from the sick room. It was from Gill. 'I forgot to tell you that Professor Keys is the chief guest on high table on Friday, so a three-part grace would really impress him.' Professor Ivor Keys – or Ivory Keys as we used to call him – was the aptly named Professor of Music. I would obviously have to do some research into Palestrina's style of composition!

So it came to pass that on the fifth day a three-part grace in the style of Palestrina composed in the form of a round, was sung in the presence of the Great One. And behold – he said it was very good. And in an atypical display of humility I did not claim copyright, but attributed the music to Gill and assured Professor Keys that I would pass on his comments. Gill was suitable grateful and became one of my best friends. Five years later she was to be my chief bridesmaid.

Gill also enrolled me into the University operatic society for their performance of Schubert's 'The Conspirators' in which I was cast as a medieval lady who had to sweep across the stage clutching a pet cat. The latter was soon made in the vacation from dried rabbit skins. My long gown did not appear in the dressing room until the night of the first performance. It was burgundy velvet, with a very high back and very low front. It was so décolleté that I decided to clutch the revolting smelling rabbit-skin cat to my somewhat exposed bosom. All went well during the singing of the chorus. Then it was time to sweep across the stage. I caught my foot in the dress – which was far too long – and my bosom-covering cat slid into the footlights. As I bent to retrieve it I received rapturous applause from the male students on the front row. At the end of the show the wardrobe mistress pointed out that I had my dress on back to front. It actually had a high front, a low back and a substantial train. The engineering students on the front row of the second night's performance were sadly disappointed.

On leaving school my headmistress had warned me not to join too many societies. I think that she knew I would work hard, but she was concerned that I would be unable to resist the plethora of opportunities to dabble in new ventures. At the Freshers' conference the stalls were set out alphabetically. I signed on immediately for the Anglican Society, and had no difficulty in moving on around the room, resisting the appeal of the Archaeological, Architectural, and Anthropological Societies.

The first stall in the 'Bs' was Bell-ringing, and on hearing I had been a ringer for three years at two ten-bell towers in Beverley I was immediately grabbed and found myself agreeing to be at the ringing practice on the following Thursday.

Onto the 'Cs' where I could, with a clear conscience, pass the Catholic Society, and not feel guilty at declining the advances of the Chemists. Round the next corner the Christians were lying in wait; the Christian Union seemed over-earnest, but the Christian Association enticed me with the offer of a free trip to Southwell Minster followed by a strawberry tea with the Bishop. A rather dishy theological student called Brian was signing up for this. I had no hesitation in following suit.

By now I was throwing caution to the winds, and as I approached the 'Ds' I heard a jaunty tune being played on an accordion. My feet were already tripping lightly as I gravitated towards the Dance Society. My mother had been the accompanist for country dancing, and from early childhood I had gone along with her and 'filled in' when needed to complete a set. So I could *pas-de-bas* and *do-si-do* before I was six, and a grand chain and figure of eight held no terrors for me. I was easy prey for the folk dancers. By now I realised I had filled my Wednesday evenings as well as my Thursday evenings. Perhaps I had better leave it at that.

I had in fact chosen well. The Anglican Society widened my vision of worship by visiting a wide range of churches each Sunday evening – some 'high', where the incense made me cough; some 'low' where they sang lots of choruses and even clapped their hands, and some 'middle of the road' from whence I had come, and to which I still incline. With the bell-ringers I rang my first (and only!) quarter peal of Bob Minor to celebrate the birth of a child in the vicarage family, and with the Christian Association I attended lively lectures by Prof. Alan Richardson, Dr. Richard Hanson and other eminent theologians, went to Methodist rallies and Quaker meetings, and walked round the university lake each Monday lunchtime in Lent to share in a famine lunch of cheese and bread, giving the price of a meal to help the hungry.

It was Wednesday evenings, however, that gave me the most pleasure. Wednesdays were good days all round, as we had lectures only in the morning. For most students the afternoon was free. Not so for Social Administration students who had to go on 'visits'. We groaned when we heard that this was to be our lot, but in fact we enjoyed our trips to schools, hospitals, remand homes, children's homes, iron works, coalmines, and most of all to factories where we were invariably given a free tea and often a free sample of their products. 'Boots the Chemists' were the most generous – Sir Jesse Boot being a great benefactor of Nottingham University. There were only three men on our course and on our Boots trip they received blue toilet bags with toothpaste and after-shave, while the girls eagerly seized their pink bags full of Number 7 cosmetics.

The evening meal on Wednesdays was high tea, which appealed to my Yorkshire appetite, and into which I tucked with enthusiasm, as I knew that any excess calories would soon be burnt off by a two-hour session of folk dancing. A bearded engineering student accompanied us on his accordion – *Nottingham Swing, Morpeth Rant, Cumberland Square Eight,* and then onto Scottish jigs and graceful Strathspeys. So keen did I become that I even spent part of my grant on some black material and made a circular skirt, which would billow out during the swings. It was the era of waists pinched in with waspie belts, and skirts, which stuck out over paper nylon petticoats. To keep these crisp it was necessary to soak them in sugar solution. The fashion did not last long, owing to the fact that if you got sweaty, then the petticoat started to get tacky, and your legs became steadily more sugary.

One Wednesday evening a group of Ukrainian men arrived at our folk dance meeting. They hadn't come to join in our dances but had come to recruit suitably sized ladies to dance with them. Arriving in the UK as refugees in the 1950s, they had found work and settled in Nottingham, and were keen to keep their tradition of dance. The only trouble was that their women-folk were busy producing babies, and hadn't the time or energy to dance, or the figures to fit into the beautiful satin costumes. Where could women dancers be found? First stop was the University Folk Dance Society. Preference was given to girls with dark hair, 24-inch waists, and heart-shaped faces. What a good job I had danced off those excess calories!

At the next Inter-varsity folk dance festival there was a feast of English, Scottish and Irish dancing, but the pièce-de-résistance was Nottingham's Ukrainian Dance team. The refugees had taught our men students to do amazing Cossack movements, with gymnastic kicks and impressive leaps. While they recovered and regained their breath for the finale, the girls took centre stage in their richly embroidered blouses, satin bodices, high red leather boots and flowered head-dresses from which flowed multi-coloured satin ribbons. The accordions and fiddles energized us with their folk melodies, as we took our partners for the final sequence and awaited the tumultuous applause.

When asked 'what did you learn at university?' I answer 'Ukrainian dancing'. I have never forgotten the steps, and surprised both my fellow holidaymakers and myself some forty years later at an evening barbecue in Poland. In a clearing in a forest a bonfire was lit and a violinist started to play. On hearing the tune of my favourite Ukrainian dance, *Hopak*, I abandoned my food, and in the light of the fire danced my heart out in a breathless flurry of fast footwork, to the utter amazement of the rest of the 'Explore' group who were considerably younger than me. Here, near to the Ukraine border, I felt a connectedness with the earth, and its rhythm. The dance took over my being and I was possessed by its positive unrelenting beat. The fiddler ran over with tears in his eyes, scarcely able to believe that an English woman in her late 50s should recognise this tune from his native country of the Ukraine, let alone be able to dance to it. Five minutes later, when I had recovered enough breath after my frenzied fire-lit footwork, I explained where I had learned *Hopak*, and felt humbled that in those far-off Nottingham days, I had played a tiny part in keeping alive part of the rich tradition of his country.

What a good job I had not heeded my headmistress's advice to limit myself to joining two, or at the most, three societies! Otherwise I would never have got round to the Ds and started a lifelong love of dancing. And what a good job I started going round the stalls clockwise. I could have gone the other way round and finished up joining the Zoology, Yoga and X-rated film society, which would never have done for an incipient vicar's wife!

Chapter Eight

Despite the counter-attractions of university life I actually did some work! Social administration, social structure, statistics, and psychology were topics that appealed more that my subsidiary subject – economics. However, by virtue of getting reasonable marks for the mathematical content and the paper on economic history, I managed to pass the part 1 exams at the end of my second year.

Social Administration students were not idle during the vacations; they were expected to do practical work. The first Easter vacation was spent in Burton's tailors in Walkden, near Bolton. I had thought I would be working in the personnel department, but in fact I enjoyed a much wider experience. First I was put with the new intake of machinists, and had to learn to thread up and operate fast electric sewing machines, following outlines of straight lines, corners and curves on tissue paper on top of cloth. Despite having a father as a tailor I had not excelled at sewing, probably because my sister Beryl had a real aptitude for it, and I could not compete. Now, with my companions being complete novices, my competitive instincts were on full alert, and I surprised my teachers, myself, (and later on, my father) by what I achieved. I even graduated to sewing pocket linings. Some days I scrubbed floors, observed life in the first aid department (many needles in fingers and one horrid cutting accident) and served hundreds of 'beans on barm cakes' for lunch in the canteen. I had to clock in at 7.30 a.m. and work full hours, which gave me valuable experience of factory work in the late 1950s.

Living and working for three weeks in a London settlement was another eye-opener. Many groups came in daily – old folks, handicapped, and unemployed. I learned to play, but never to enjoy, whist and bingo, and I was sent on missions to prisons, hospitals and slums. At one tenement I rang the appropriate bell, and a haggard old lady opened a sash window on the third floor and dropped down her door key, suspended on the end of a length of wool, in the style of Rapunzel letting down her golden hair. At another flat where I was trying to help a single mother with three children to sort out her finances, there was a knock at the door. I never saw who was there, as the children scarpered, and the mother caught hold of my cardigan and dragged me behind the settee with instructions not to make a noise. We lay there cowering, and in my mind I envisaged men with guns about to break down the door. When the banging stopped, the children shouted 'He's gone' and mother proceeded to put on the kettle.

'Could have been the landlord wanting the rent', she said. 'Haven't got it.'

'Could have been the youngest kid's dad'. Last time he threatened me with a carving knife. You will stay and have a cuppa, won't you?'

I was a coward, and declined. Social work theory and practice were two different things!

I did not really enjoy my settlement experiences, but I was grateful for my one Saturday off, as it coincided with the last night of the Proms. Fellow student Jill and I borrowed collapsible canvas stools and took up our pitch in the long queue snaking the Royal Albert Hall waiting for returned tickets. The camaraderie of the crowd was superb; we shared food, told jokes and sang a wide variety of songs – many of them way outside our usual repertoire! As the September sun disappeared we began to shiver. A Scotsman came to our rescue with 'a bit of something to warm the cockles of your bonnie hearts'. It certainly burned our throats and cast off a few inhibitions. At twenty minutes past seven, when we were beginning to doubt the wisdom of spending over eight hours on the pavement, we were offered two promenade tickets, wiggled our way to the front of the hall, and appeared on TV to amazed family and friends waving our university scarves with gay abandon to the strains of *Rule Britannia.*

After further holiday stints in Youth employment, Education department and hospitals I knew where my sympathies lay, and which career path I wanted to follow. Industry and local authorities were not my scene; hospitals were. I would train as a hospital almoner. First I had to get my degree. And I nearly didn't!

The first of my finals had gone well. The second exam - Human growth and development - was an afternoon one starting at 2 p.m. and finishing at 5 p.m. As it was a sunny morning I decided to do my last minute revision by the university lake, but the distraction of 'the rest of the world' who could enjoy messing about in boats, was too great. I gathered up my files and made for the new Social Science library. I thought it was strange that no one else from our year was there. Half an hour later, around eleven o'clock, an urgent voice invaded the silence.

'Has anyone seen Miss Jefferson? She hasn't reported for her half past nine exam.'

I had obviously misread the exam timetable!

In the ensuing blur I confessed to being the culprit, was led over to the main building, taken up to the exam room in the library lift, armed with a pen and exam paper and told that I had an hour and a half in which to complete the three hour exam paper. Luckily for me no students had come out of the exam room for toilet or any other reason. Otherwise I would have not been allowed in.

I decided I must try to answer all four questions, even if it meant writing in note form rather than flowing prose. My luck was definitely in – the first question was: 'Describe how the human being copes with stress…'

My adrenalin kicked in. I wrote with feeling!

My tutor was waiting for me outside the exam room. He had been so worried about my absence that he had been to my 'digs' where the landlady had told him I had left in good spirits with my gown on my arm at half past eight. He had then been to see the university chaplain, who assured him I had been at morning prayers, and that I was not seemingly the suicidal type. I had always wondered what they did with the passport type photos you had to give in on registration day. Mine had come in useful when the university authorities had issued my description to both Nottingham City and Nottingham County police. I was touched by everyone's concern. I was also, by now, distinctly sick and shaky and convinced that I had said goodbye to prospects of getting a degree. I said as much in a 9-page letter to my fiancé, Michael, bewailing my predicament. Selfishly I had not thought of the effect of this letter on his morale on the eve of his own finals – but I had to tell someone, and parents were not the ones to know. Not yet!

My tutor came to collect me in his car for the two remaining exams. I had, of course, double checked the exam timetable this time, and knew exactly when they were. After they were over I relaxed by watching the Derby on TV, and the next day went to Boston in Lincolnshire to my musician friend Gill's home. The normality of life in a market town, going shopping, helping at 'The Welfare' where Gill's mum weighed babies, and playing simple non-mind-stretching games, like snakes and ladders were the welcome antidote to the stress of the preceding days.

Gill's house, like ours, had an outside toilet. It had no light. As I never had to 'go' in the night I did not concentrate on what Gill's dad was saying about where they kept the torch. Inevitably that night I did want to go. There was no chamber pot under the bed, so I crept downstairs, unlocked the back door and groped my way around a wall until I found a door. I had no slippers on, and thought the floor was rather bumpy. Another step further in and I was in the middle of the coal heap. I groped for the second door and opened the latch. The lavender smell was promising. I felt for the chain, turned round and was relieved.

My screams, followed by hysterical laughter, awoke not only Gill's dad, but also the next-door neighbour who shone a torch down onto the back yard, where I stood with a wet nightie clinging to my legs. Gill's toilet was more sophisticated than ours. It had a lid, which was left in the closed position. This had been my downfall. Gill and her mother and sister came down to see what all the noise was about, supplied me with a dry nightie and put the kettle on for a midnight tea party. Exam results seemed a million miles away.

Results day proved that my adrenalin rush on exam day must have been effective; I had gained an Upper Two degree. At the graduation I fairly tripped up the steps to the stage of the Albert Hall in Nottingham, wearing a borrowed pair of black court shoes, and the stipulation 'black dress', which I had bought from a jumble sale for two shillings. At the strawberry tea in Florence Boot hall after the ceremony I saw my tutor approaching. Like it or not I knew I had to reveal all to my parents before he joked about my late appearance in the examination room. I could not believe how unconcerned they were about the affair. I still have nightmares about missing exams and appointments, and am obsessed with daily diary checking – not only with the one in my handbag, but also with my palmtop. And when reading a timetable I put a straight edge against the line I am following so that my eyes don't stray onto the line below!

After my post-graduate year in Newcastle, working firstly in the Northumberland Children's department and then in Dryburn Hospital in Durham, I qualified as a hospital almoner, and took up my first post at the Royal Hospital in Sheffield.

I survived one of the coldest winters of that century (1962/3) having to walk to work when the buses stopped, and having to carry water from my landlady's basement to my cold attic flat to flush the loo.

The head almoner, Helen, asked if I would be willing to act as supervisor for a social work student on her practical work placement. I readily agreed and was bemused to find that Alice was, in fact, an undergraduate at Nottingham. I decided it would not be a good idea to mention that I had graduated from there only two years previously. It was better for her to think that I was an almoner with years of medical social work experience behind me. She showed promise, and at the end of her six-week stint I called her into my office to wish her well. I could not resist the rejoinder to make sure that when she did her finals she read the exam timetable thoroughly and was at the exam room in good time.

'Oh yes, I will' she assured me, 'Dr. Emerson told us an awful tale about a girl who got confused and didn't turn up for her finals.

'Goodness,' I exclaimed, 'what on earth happened?'

'Well, they went to her digs, they rang the police, they talked to the chaplain, and they even talked of dredging the lake.'

I was intrigued by how the story was unfolding, and how it had been embroidered.

'And what happened to this girl – did she get her degree?' I asked.

'I don't know.' said Alice. 'I hope so. I wonder what she went on to do?'

'Actually she got an Upper Two, and she became a hospital almoner.'

'She didn't get a job at Sheffield Royal, did she?' ventured Alice, who was rapidly cottoning on.

'Come to think of it, I do believe she did.'

Victory in Europe fancy dress celebration on Beverley racecourse.
May 1945. Author 2nd from left, as 'Red Riding Hood'. The hood
must have blown away as only the basket is left!

Beverley High School Sixth form. 1957.
Author seated on extreme right.

Nottingham University's Ukrainian dance team. 1961
Author second step up on the right.

Michael adjusts Margaret's veil outside St. Mary's church, Beverley
October 1963. (Courtesy Yorkshire Post Newspapers)

*Sheba, the Golden Labrador/cross, desecrating or rebuilding a
Pennine dry stone wall.*

'Pinza the Stealer' - Our second rescue dog.

Crepello, the chipmunk who lived in the bathroom in Llangollen.

Michael with one of Rhian's puppies in Kerry.

Chapter Nine

No animals were allowed in my attic flat, so the only contact I had with them was on home visits, when I was checking how patients were coping after being discharged from hospital. As I rang people's doorbells I prayed hard that a soft feline would greet me and not a barking Labrador; I still had a fear of dogs, and when seated in a canine household I would barricade my ankles and legs with carefully positioned briefcase and handbag.

Mrs Smith didn't have a cat or a dog, but she had an elderly parrot that talked. It resented my intrusion and set up a counter attack of babble, which it continued even when she threw a tablecloth over its cage.

'Talk proper for the hospital lady' shouted my client, who proudly told me he could say 'God bless the Queen' and 'would you like a cup of tea?'

The parrot sulked and became silent for the rest of my visit. However, just as I was leaving he became very excited and screeched, 'God bless a cup of tea' and 'would you like the Queen?'

I left the dyslexic parrot to go on to visit an old man in Attercliffe to ascertain how he was getting on after his eye operation. Being from Yorkshire myself I was well attuned to the dialect, but on this occasion had great difficulty in understanding a word the old man was saying. After several 'pardons' and 'I'm sorry, I didn't quite catch that' on my part, the old man confessed that he would do better with his teeth in. The trouble was – he couldn't find where he had put them. I gathered he normally soaked them in a glass of water overnight, but on searching the bathroom and bedroom I drew a blank. I didn't make much headway either with the conversation. Mercifully he went out to the kitchen to make me a cup of tea. It was then that I spied the goldfish bowl. Two handsome fat fish were swimming over a pink and cream arched bridge. I lowered my hand into the bowl, retrieved both sets of teeth and removed the weed before handing them to a delighted owner. I wrote in my notes 'Patient very cheerful, but will cope better when he gets his new specs!'

During my year as hospital almoner in Sheffield, Michael was in his final year at St. Aidan's Theological College in Birkenhead. We were saving up to get married as soon as he was ordained deacon. My salary was not large, and Michael was on a student grant. He therefore hitch-hiked everywhere, and on one of his free afternoons he was lucky with his lifts and arrived at my hospital well before my finishing time of 5.30 p.m. It was a cold and wet November afternoon, so he decided to find a warm place in the hospital to settle down to doing some revision for the dreaded Greek exam. He wandered through to the outpatients waiting area, where the WVS ladies were selling cups of tea for 2d. and unfortunately sat down on a chair in the psychiatric department. He was wearing a large grey duffel coat and looked as if he was in need of a shave. After a few minutes of trying to revise Greek in a very warm hospital, sleep overcame him and his head slumped.

My report writing was interrupted by a staff nurse from outpatients who said she needed my help.

'We've just finished the psychiatric clinic,' she said, ' but there's a strange young bloke asleep on the chairs. He's not on our list – I think he's a tramp who's come in for the warmth. Can you come and deal with him? I don't suppose he's got a bed for the night.'

I followed her back to outpatients and knew at once what the tramp needed.

'Leave it with me' I said to the nurse. 'I happen to know this one. And I'll soon sort him out.'

I proceeded to prod Michael, and before he could embrace me and give the game away I commanded him, in an authoritative voice, to come with me to my office, where I would sort out his problems. Meek as a lamb he followed me to my department, where we had a most pleasant and intimate interview until the end of the afternoon. Fancy being paid for entertaining my fiancé!

I did find him a bed. No – it wasn't mine – but a single one on the ground floor where my landlady could ascertain that there was no 'hanky-panky'. Michael seemed to charm my landladies both in Nottingham and Sheffield; the fact that he was an ordinand lent him an air of gravitas and utter respectability in their eyes.

I had wondered what was in the big carrier bag that my somnolent tramp had stowed under his psychiatric department chair. It was a present for me in the form of a somewhat battered Dansette record player. Apparently a fellow student was feeling a financial pinch, so to raise enough money to travel home at the end of term he sold the Dansette to Michael for £2. I was very touched by this gift, as I loved music, and could see that my dear fiancé had also bought me a record to play. He said I must wait until he had gone before opening it, and he hoped I would like this surprise.

Would he have remembered that I liked Beethoven? Or was it Chopin's piano music, as he had heard me practising *Waltz no.2 in C sharp minor* in the holidays? On the other hand it could be something romantic – maybe a selection of love songs. Through the rather flimsy paper I thought I could discern the word SHARP. So perhaps it was the Chopin waltz after all. As soon as I had gone up to my attic flat after a rather tearful farewell I tore open the paper and pulled out a pink record sleeve with a four letter title: SHAP under which was a picture of a steam locomotive.

Until I received my next pay packet that was the only record I had to play. It was an LP (long playing record) with such exciting sounds as the engine steaming up, the engine puffing and panting as it climbed Shap, and the engine cruising once it was over the Cumbrian summit. If I hadn't drifted off to sleep before side number one had ended I had the thrill of turning the record over to hear more diddle-di-dee's and chuffity-chuffs, but I knew the end was mercifully near when I heard the only non-railway sound – a cuckoo! This record was a kind thought – but it made me wonder how often do we give gifts that we ourselves would like to have received rather than ones which would give pleasure to the recipient? On his next visit Michael redeemed himself by bringing me another LP that started with *'Ich liebe dich'* the strains of which my landlady much preferred to the railway noises that had, for two months, pervaded her domain.

Back in Sheffield Royal Hospital I continued to enjoy my job on the ophthalmic and surgical wards, where one of the consultants was unfortunately named Mr Darke! I marvel now when friends are in and out of hospital in a morning, having had a cataract removed. In the early 1960s patients who had eye operations had big bandages swathing their faces and had to lie very still for an inordinate length of time. They were very grateful if I had time to chat to them after I had ascertained what help they were going to need on discharge. On men's surgical wards I listened patiently to intimate details of the horrors of 'passing a motion' after an operation for piles. Even today at committee meetings I cringe when the chairperson asks if we can pass a motion, for experience has shown that this can be almost as painful an experience!

I worked mainly with the registrars and housemen on each of my ophthalmic and surgical 'firms'. Only occasionally did I get to see the consultant, and this was usually on the weekly ward rounds when I was invited to attend along with the physiotherapist and occupational therapist. There was always a flap on the wards before the ward round. Sister, in her navy blue dress and starched cap, and staff nurse in her lilac dress chivvied the lesser mortals of the nursing hierarchy to fill up the water jugs, remove newspapers and see that all beds had the statutory hospital corners clearly in evidence.

Most doctors had good rapport with both their patients and the ancillary staff, but a few tapped and poked their patients with grim expressions on their faces, revealing not a vestige of hope. Sometimes they would then carry on, with the medical students, a whispered discussion of the prognosis and possible treatment, and completely ignore the rest of us. We – and the poor patient – were kept in ignorance.

There was one ward where I feared going. The ward sister was reputedly a real battle-axe and she was certainly not tolerant of almoners, whom she considered a waste of time. In many ways ward sisters were more influential than anyone else in the hospital, bar the consultant, and long-standing ward sisters could even dare to over-rule newly-qualified consultants. My 'boss' therefore was forced to accept that on one particular female surgical ward there were to be no 'hangers-on' to the ward rounds.

When I needed to visit that ward I tried to do it when Sister was off duty, and the pleasant staff nurse was in charge. Three months into my new job and I timed it wrong; sister was on duty. It was etiquette always to ask for permission to go on her ward to see a patient. I knocked timorously at her office door. No response. Looking through the glass I saw that she was at her desk with her head in her hands. Fearing that she was ill I bravely walked in and asked if she was all right. To my surprise she did not snap back and send me scuttling away. Her eyes were red and moist; she looked utterly washed out. She looked suddenly so vulnerable and I instinctively reached out to her and asked if she wanted to tell me what was the matter.

'I'm just so worn out,' she said. 'I don't know how long I can go on like this. I'm on my own at home trying to care for my mother who has dementia. Last night she got out of the house and was found wandering. The police brought her back, and by the time I'd got her back into bed it was time to come to work. Now I can't concentrate on the paper work, and I keep wondering if the neighbour has gone in to get mother some lunch.'

I had gone to that ward to see Mrs Mason in bed number three, In fact she was not to be my patient that afternoon; it was the Ward sister who needed my listening ear. It was clearly a release for her to tell me her hitherto pent up feelings. She admitted that she had never told any of her nursing staff for fear of appearing weak. Eventually she agreed to my talking to them and to the medical team. In addition I was able to help by organising meals-on-wheels for her mother, a weekly outing to the day care centre, and friendly visits by ladies from a local church.

From then on I was never afraid of going on to that ward; indeed I was even offered a cup of tea in sister's office. I had thought that the icing on the proverbial cake was the news that sister had told the consultant that she thought it would be a good idea for the almoner to join the ward round. However, what touched me more was a request from sister to go to her office on my final day working in that hospital. The battle-axe actually kissed me and gave me an exquisite cut glass flower vase as a wedding present.

I still use it and treasure it. It is a constant reminder that too often we judge people unjustly, not knowing their circumstances. When I look at the flowers in that vase I also think of how 'closed up' that ward sister was – never divulging any of her worries to those around her. Only when she was encouraged to see that sharing them with her fellow workers would help both herself and her staff, did she flower and reveal the true and very caring person she really was underneath her starched hat.

Chapter Ten

If you thought the era of paying a 'bride price' had long since gone, then you are mistaken. Michael decided to do the correct thing and ask my father for his daughter's hand in marriage. To get a private hearing he went into our shop on the pretext of buying two pairs of underpants. He knew from experience that at the end of a transaction father would always ask hopefully, 'anything more?'

Sure enough, when the underpants had been bought, wrapped in brown paper and tied up with string, father said to Michael 'anything more?'

Michael's reply was unexpected - 'Yes, your daughter!' So I was sold along with two pairs of Y fronts.

I enjoyed every aspect of my wedding preparations. During our long courtship I had ample time in which to find the engagement ring that suited both my hand and our budget. The resulting Victorian gold ring with recessed tiny diamonds and sapphires fitted the bill – which came to £4.10s. When one of the stones came out, many years later, the jeweller informed me that they were only glass. He expected me to be horror-stricken, but I told him I had long suspected that, but would not change the ring for all the tea in China. My wedding ring cost twice as much as my engagement ring, but costs were cut when I found some pearly white 'Ottoman Tricel' bridal material in Sheffield market. It was an 'end of roll' bargain, and allowed for a high-necked, long sleeved dress with a long floating train, which a lady in a back street in Beverley made up for me for the very modest cost of £1.10s. I also bought a very long tulle veil, a pearly coronet and pointed white stiletto heeled shoes (for as yet I had no bunion!)

In the early 1960s the wedding list was a list of invited guests, rather than a list of 'must-haves' for the ideal home. As I was marrying the vicar's son this list was a diplomatic nightmare. Invite one churchwarden and you had to invite the other three. The organist was on the list – but what about the verger? We left our parents to sort out the politics. I was still working as an almoner in Sheffield, and Michael was preparing for his ordination, which was just a month before the wedding. His ordination solved one problem – that of what Michael should wear for the wedding. We decided that a brand new cassock would look splendid and obviate the need for spending our limited resources on a wedding suit.

When my sister was married my father told her that it would have to be on a Bank Holiday Monday, as he did not wish to shut his shop on Saturday, which was his most lucrative sales day. Perhaps the only time father showed any favouritism to me was allowing me to be wed on a Saturday. The shop counter flap was put back so that I could emerge through the front shop door, which was festooned with men's working socks, and Tootal ties. This time I could sit on the back seat of a taxi and not on the fold down one, and wave, like the Queen, to the people of Holme Church Lane who stood on the corner to 'see me off'.

As we approached St. Mary's church I fondly imagined that Michael would be in position in the front pew kneeling in prayer. Instead he was outside church doing a deal with a college friend, involving car headlights and other spare parts. The best man ushered him into church in the nick of time, but even as father and I stood at the west door ready for the grand entrance, Michael leapt from his pew and went up the pulpit steps. Good heavens – was he about to give a sermon?

No – he had rigged up in the pulpit a tape recorder, and just in time he had remembered to switch it on.

I swept up the long aisle of the ancient church, and in a beautiful service Margaret Jefferson became Margaret Walker, and the tailor's daughter became the curate's wife. The bells, which once we had rung together, rang out a touch of Grandsire Triples across the market town as we posed for a few photos (black and white in those days) and were driven to the reception at the tannery social club. Wedding receptions were usually very modest affairs in the early 1960s, and although we had 120 guests the meal was really only afternoon tea. Ladies of the parishes had made cucumber sandwiches, ham sandwiches and egg sandwiches, and had baked sausage rolls, scones and butterfly buns. They went from table to table wielding huge brown teapots, as tea was the only drink available apart from the glass of port to accompany the speeches and the cake.

The wedding cake was our present from my parents; it was square and three-tiered, and royal iced with intricately fine trelliswork interspersed with silver horseshoes. Presiding from the top was a small silver vase of lilies-of the valley.

Leaving the guests to converse, Michael and I were driven to his father's vicarage to get changed into our 'going-away outfits', for in those days the receptions were thankfully short and did not metamorphose into evening affairs with dancing until the early hours. Michael doffed his cassock, while I put on my red bouclé suit with a squirrel collar. I had no choice of whether I should wear a hat or not. I had to wear the cream one my mother had bought to go with her wedding outfit. This colour did nothing for her, and did not show up on her white hair. The day before the wedding my sister decreed that she should get a brighter one. The shop would not take the white one back, so I averted a potentially tearful situation by declaring that it would go splendidly with my going away suit.

Back at the tannery club we kissed hordes of relatives and friends, then turned to the 'going away car' which, in our absence, had been decorated with tin cans and whitewashed with 'FROM HERE TO MATERNITY' on either side. My brother, home from Canada, the best man and a tribe of nephews and half cousins had surely had a hand in this. Nine months later they were to realise the truth that slogan contained!

★★★★★★★★★★★★★★★

Any ideas of getting a cat were put on hold when we knew a baby was on the way. All the baby books warned of the dangers of cats jumping onto prams and suffocating the occupants. They also advocated putting baby in the pram after daytime feeds, to enjoy the fresh air and sunshine, whatever the temperature, so mothers had to invest in gauze nets to string across the pram to inhibit curious moggies.

Christopher was therefore safe from predators as he lay in his Silver Cross coach built pram which we bought second hand for £8 from our neighbours on the housing estate in York, where Michael was serving his first curacy. However, other beasts lay in wait for our son and heir. He had been put into his wicker treasure cot after his six o'clock evening feed and had eventually gone to sleep. Curled up on the sofa, reading Dr. Spock's bible of childcare, I heard a blood-curdling scream from above. Michael, who had been toiling over a sermon in the small bedroom, which served as his study, ran into Christopher's room to see blood pouring from our baby's neck. As he picked Christopher up he saw a long furry creature with its sharp teeth still clinging onto the cot blanket. I was shaking as Michael passed the baby to me and then prised the vicious animal from the bedclothes, seized it by its neck and threw it out onto the front lawn.

We learned later that the man in the house next but one to ours had lost his prize ferret. I had no sympathy. We had nearly lost our prize baby.

Money was not plentiful in 1964. The curate's stipend was £500, although Michael had an extra £50 for being part-time hospital chaplain. However we had the big advantage of a 'free house' and a church-owned gas cooker. We had also arrived in York with an enormous array of wedding presents. I can recommend marrying a vicar's son, as I am sure many of Michael's father's parishioners thought that they would earn a quick passage to heaven by giving us fine wedding gifts. Not that our expectations were great – for it was presumed that you would build up your home gradually. There was no thought of starting married life with such things as washing machines, fridges, televisions or vacuum cleaners. These came with age! Wedding gifts were much more modest and from the list which I still possess I see that we received 32 pairs of pillowcases, 12 towels, 3 blankets, much cutlery, china and kitchenware, several vases, lots of Pyrex dishes and a mound of hand embroidered tablecloths with serviettes – presumably for vicarage tea parties.

As our house was brand new we were told to wait for a year until the plaster had dried out before we started wallpapering. We had bought some patterned paper for the lounge – gold cockerels subtlety interwoven into a regency design. I was itching to prove my decorating skills, learned from my father, but as I nearly always seemed to be feeding the baby, bringing up his wind or changing nappies, Michael made his maiden voyage into home décor. He was doing very well and I was impressed that he insisted on switching off the electricity while he unscrewed the light switch when he came to papering that corner of the room. With just one piece to paste up on that wall before bedtime, he finished it with a flourish, switched the electricity on from the mains and came immediately up to bed. The next morning I was the first to come downstairs. The papering by the light switch was immaculately done, but the length of paper in the far corner looked different from the rest.

The cockerels were standing on their heads, and presumably calling 'doo-doodle-a-cock'!

From home decorating we proceeded to tackle the garden. Being the end plot the builders had thrown lots of rubble onto it so we were advised to plant potatoes to clear the soil. So in went the Arran Pilot and the Majestic varieties and they both flourished. My father told us we should bank them up to encourage a good crop. We were disconcerted to find that the two rows nearest the boundary fence had all their tops missing. Our garden backed onto fields, and the previous week we had noticed that horses had been brought in. We were cross, at the time, that they had been feasting on our embryo crop, but a neighbour informed us – (rightly or wrongly we know not) that one of the horses was Harvey Smith's 'Harvester'. We followed this horse's progress with interest and when he achieved international medals we knew that his success was undoubtedly due to his harvesting of the illicit tops of the Walkers' first potato crop!

Chapter Eleven

'I am quite happy living in the curate's house,' said Leslie, the vicar of Michael's second curacy, in the dockland area of East Hull. 'So I trust that you are happy to move into the vicarage'. As Leslie was a bachelor and as we already had one baby, and another on the way, it seemed a sensible arrangement. We loved the Edwardian house with its three large reception rooms and five bedrooms. What we did find difficult was furnishing and heating it on Michael's modest stipend. Reluctantly we sold some of our wedding presents to keep solvent and I determined to become an expert in economic cookery.

Thanks to my wartime upbringing I already had a book full of recipes made from cheap ingredients. Today's generation would probably turn their noses up at delicacies such as brawn, faggots and pigs' trotters and would undoubtedly retch at the prospect of taking the skin off a pig's tongue. My only failure was with cooking brains from the sheep's head, which the butcher sold to me for a shilling. The resultant grey sludge could in no way be described as an appetiser. Its destiny was the waste bin.

Expensive branded cleaning ingredients rarely found their way into the vicarage cupboards; instead I resorted to a precious little book commending the use of vinegar and lemon juice. Past copies of the Hull Daily Mail came in useful for polishing the windows, bread was rubbed onto wallpaper to removed dirty marks, and after a meeting in the church hall it was very liberating to throw the dregs of tea leaves onto the wooden floor. Any dust stuck to the soggy tealeaves and could then easily be swept away.

One problem that was harder to solve was how to get an owl out of your dining room. Michael had gone off to an all day meeting somewhere in West Hull. Eight months pregnant and with a two-year-old son playing happily in the front room I was just enjoying a third cup of tea before clearing away the breakfast things, when there was a terrible kafuffle in the chimney breast, followed by a squawk and a frantic fluttering of sooty wings as an owl descended onto the hearth. Two penetrating eyes rotated to size up the scene, then this monstrous bird, which stood over a foot tall and had a wingspan of over three feet, took off across the table. Its chest feathers stuck to the marmalade jar, which it skimmed on its route to the windowsill. I opened the back door in the hope that it would smell fresh air and depart. No such luck. The wise bird found the ascending warm flow of air from the convector heater much more to its liking.

The owl eyed me condescendingly from its new perch on top of the curtain rail. Now that it was off the windowsill I could open the window. As if to punish me for this unexpected blast of cold air the owl swooped onto my head before taking off again to bask in the convector heater's blast. I was shaking with fear; my unborn baby was panicking too and kicking violently. I ran out of the room and banged the door behind me, and I remember feeling guilty for leaving the heater on when the windows and back door were open. What a waste of heat! I had no near neighbours and my husband and vicar were at a meeting somewhere the other side of Hull. What should I do? Who would deal with a tawny owl who fancied himself as a chimney sweep and who had a voracious appetite for marmalade and my hair? Why – the RSPCA of course. I would phone them.

It was then I realised I had not seen Christopher for some time. I went upstairs; he was not in the bedrooms. Then from the attic I heard urgent screams. Lumping my fat body up the narrow steps I found Christopher under Michael's Hornby Dublo railway layout. This was definitely a 'no unattended children allowed' area. I prayed hard that he had not meddled with any of the locos. But he hadn't, for he was well and truly impounded on some wiring on the underside of the layout. With great difficulty I crawled over the splintery floorboards to reach him, and successfully unhooked him. As he made for the attic stairs I turned to crawl after him, only to find that now I too was caught up on the wiring. I cursed, Christopher cried, and far down below I heard 'Tee-whit- tee woo'.

I prayed to St. Francis, patron saint of birds and animals, and then to St. Jude, patron saint of lost causes. Their answer was clear and obvious. Take off the sweater and leave it clawed by wires, and emerge semi-topless to sort out child and owl. The RSPCA man was round a few minutes later, armed with a net and a large cage. I was not allowed in to observe his technique, but he soon emerged triumphant with an imprisoned blackened bird. I thanked him profusely, stared at the blinking owl who reciprocated with a recriminating ogle. I turned to ask the RSPCA man what he would do with the owl, but found that he was staring too – at me.

Maybe he thought that it was an idiosyncrasy of my pregnancy that I went round on cold February mornings in a bra and vest!

After the birth of our second baby, Pauline, in 1967, we bought a tent so that we could enjoy cheap camping holidays. After a few days in Kielder Forest in Northumberland we gravitated to the coast to a fairly empty campsite at Beadnell. One day we stopped to shop for food and as the lady in front of us filled her shopping bag with tins of dog food, Michael and I looked at one another and afterwards agreed that when there was so much famine and starvation in the world it was morally and ethically wrong to spend so much money on keeping a dog. On our return to the campsite we were utterly amazed to find it chock-a-block with tents. Apparently it was Newcastle's holiday week! Perilously close to our tent was an identical one, whose owners had an identical car to ours – a black Ford Consul with red upholstery. They also had two children of comparable age to ours. However, they also had a dog. Horror of horrors it was a dreaded yellow Labrador. I would keep my distance.

Returning from the toilet block I was horrified to see this beast helping herself to carrots from our tent. As Michael eased her out he remarked, 'If by law I had to keep a dog, I'd have one like this – a nice big one – a proper dog.'

Words carry easily from one tent to another and immediately the Labrador's owners retaliated:

'You don't really want a dog, do you? Sheba is only 3 years old, and so well behaved. We are emigrating to South Africa at the end of the month and can't find anyone to take her. It will break our hearts to have her put down.'

That night we tossed and turned, swallowed our words about morals and ethics of pet-ownership, and in a moment of rashness agreed to pick up Sheba from their home in County Durham at the end of our holidays. As the owners said, if she didn't settle with us, then she wouldn't settle anywhere. They would pay for vet's fees if we couldn't cope and had to have her put down. We inherited the dog bowls, the lead and the 7/6d dog licence, and drove off with an unperturbed dog sitting on the back seat between the children. Michael and I were very perturbed. What had we done? Neither of us had any experience of dog ownership; I was terrified of dogs – especially Labradors; and to add to our worries was the fact that we had arranged to break our return journey at a vicarage in North Yorkshire, with David and Margaret – former colleagues in our Hull parish. With great forbearance they greeted us warmly – canine adjunct included, and recommended tiring the dog out so that she would sleep soundly and not fret. Two and a half hours later David, Michael and Sheba returned from the moors and we all slept soundly.

On our return home we opened the post. There was a letter with a Birmingham postmark, and I recognised my cousin's handwriting. Yes – it was true –in my Christmas letter I had issued a warm welcome for Pat, her husband Dennis and three children to come to stay with us in the summer. I read, with growing alarm, ' We would love to take you up on your offer, and unless we hear to the contrary we will arrive in Hull on August 3rd'. The letter had been on our doormat for twelve days. They had not heard to the contrary and would be arriving tomorrow. Coping with our new pet now seemed less pressing, as we made up beds and shopped for nine people. Sheba proved a natural with children, loved racing around the garden with them, and integrated easily into our enlarged family. Photos of our happy dog were posted out to South Africa to reassure her previous owners that there was absolutely no question of 'having Sheba put down'. And so began our lifetime as pet-owners.

Chapter Twelve

Sheba settled well into parish life, proving to be an able guard dog, while being friendly and 'pattable' to all legitimate visitors to the vicarage. People who came to book their child's baptism, to arrange their wedding or to talk over a problem with the clergy were often unbelievably nervous as they rang the vicarage doorbell. Maybe the sight of a young mum with a baby tucked under her arm, a little boy building wooden bricks and a tail-wagging happy dog did much to allay their fears as they waited for Michael to appear and put them entirely at ease.

Three years as a curate on a new estate in York, followed by three years serving three post-war estates in dockland Hull, were drawing to a close. Michael had been offered the incumbency of St. Jude's church in Halifax. His time in Hull had sometimes involved visits to the Missions to Seamen institute, and they gave him a leaving gift in the form of a glass case containing a four-foot long model of a ship. In fact it was only half a ship – the other half was reflected in a mirror, which formed the back of the case. It was probably a model built as a promotional display piece.

We regret now that we ruined it almost immediately. I had the inspired, but misguidedly foolish idea of removing the top, filling the case with water up to the Plimsoll line, and introducing our second batch of pets. The next morning there was a puddle on the floor, the ship was almost grounded, and the two floundering goldfish were gasping. Michael squirted a putty-like sealant to the corners of the glass case, but it never became watertight, and the fish had to downsize to a bowl. The boat in its putty-cornered glass case followed the antique Victorian fire screen and other non-utilitarian wedding presents to the saleroom to offset the cost of furnishing our even bigger vicarage in Halifax.

Situated opposite 73 acres of parkland, St. Jude's vicarage had been built in 1895, five years after the millstone grit church with its imposing tower. Now a residential care home for twenty old people, the vicarage then had five bedrooms on the first floor and five on the second floor, which had no heat whatsoever. Pennine winters tended to be severe so these attic rooms were never inhabited except for the tinplate passengers and livestock who stood immobile on the platforms and in the marshalling yards of Michael's railway layout. Occasionally the children would play up there. On one occasion when Michael's mother was looking after them she detected an alarming smell from the attic region. Christopher had received a chemistry set for Christmas. Who better to advise him on his experiments than Philip, son of our lay reader, who was chemistry master at the nearby grammar school?

The sound of grandma's footsteps up the attic stairs forestalled Christopher's final application of a test-tube of green powder to the explosive potential of the methylated spirit burner. Grandma turned as green as the powder, but Philip did his best to set her mind at rest:

'Don't worry, Mrs Walker. We did think it might go pop, so that's why we moved up into the attic. We started the experiment in the cellar, but I pointed out to Christopher that if it went wrong it might blow up the entire vicarage. Far better to do it in the attic, and then only the roof would be blown off.'

Philip was the sort of boy who spelt trouble, yet had a beguiling impish grin, which charmed you into a misguided confidence that his next joint exploit with your son would be utterly innocent. They spent many a Sunday afternoon exploring the sewers and culverts of the area, on the pretext of working out the parish boundaries! They both proceeded from junior school to grammar school, where they had a united hatred of cross-country running. The usual route was round Savile Park, the corner of which was marked by a fountain, clearly visible from the vicarage. On Wednesday afternoons Christopher was always seen to be bringing up the rear. This did not concern me, but it did concern Michael, who had been captain of the harriers at university in Lampeter. In an effort to encourage our son to run faster we bribed him with chocolate.

'If you are not the last runner next Wednesday we'll give you a pack of two Cadbury's creme eggs.'

We were not free to watch the next cross-country, but were reliably informed that Christopher was not last. The eggs were duly handed over. The following week the same inducement was offered. Running at the rear of the field was Christopher. Unaware of our watching eyes his friend

Philip stopped, to let Christopher overtake him for the last ten metres. Christopher could honestly claim that he was not last, and could therefore legitimately claim the two eggs, one of which was Philip's reward for initiating this cunningly hatched plan.

Christopher may never have collected cups and medals for athletic prowess, but he made up for it with a childhood full of other collections. Starting with fossils, he proceeded to collect model buses, stamps, coins, mysteriously named QSL cards (something to do with radio, I think!), and sets of Kings and Queens from one petrol station, and 3D prehistoric animals from another. We ate boxes of Weetabix to qualify for each offer – Tee shirts, excellent atlases and astronomical wall charts. Suddenly our diet changed from Weetabix to Mars Bars. Mars was running a competition involving collecting letters of the alphabet from its Mars Bar wrappers. My memory of one particular canal holiday is of going round Drayton Manor Park Zoo. I do not recall one single animal, but I could take you on a conducted tour of all the litter bins in the park, through which I had to grovel in a gooey last ditch attempt to find the much needed letters M and B for our competition entry which had to be posted that afternoon. We didn't win, but it was not for want of trying. Maybe it was because we had no glue with which to stick our letters on the grid – we had to rely solely on the 'stickability' of the caramel from the Mars Bars wrappers!

Meanwhile what was Pauline up to in her leisure time? She soon collected around her an array of little girls from the large terraced houses behind the vicarage, and they pushed their dolls' prams up and down the drive, played doctors and nurses, and tried on my hats and tottered in my high-heeled shoes in the ways that little girls do. One day I returned from a wedding, eager to finish off the job of papering our bedroom. Christopher had gone with his dad to take Sheba for a walk across the moor. I assumed that Pauline was still over at her friend's house, so without changing out of my wedding garb I mixed the paste and started applying it onto the paper rolled out on the landing floor. I was startled by the gruff voice of our Sunday school superintendent. Somewhat surprised to catch me in full wedding gear, brandishing a paste brush, she shouted:

'Do you know what your daughter is up to?'

I confessed that I thought she was at her friend Lorraine's house. Apparently she was not. She had been found struggling to push my tea trolley up the cobbled back street, laden with empty lemonade bottles, which she had taken from our neighbours' dustbins. When asked by the Sunday school lady what on earth she was doing she demonstrated her early entrepreneurial skills by showing off the three-penny bits she had amassed from the corner shop as a result of her first batch of refundable pop bottles!

We kept a closer eye on her wanderings after that. Not that she wanted to wander far in the winter months. Neither did we. After services on Sunday mornings we enjoyed warming stews in the 'back room' where there was a coke burner. If it worked flat out we could lift the temperature to 55 degrees Fahrenheit. The only time we heated the official dining room was for a fortnight over Christmas.

One Sunday afternoon was unusually peaceful. Sheba was flat out in front of the fire, Michael was in the study preparing for his hospital ward service, and Christopher and I were playing Lexicon – precursor of Scrabble. Pauline and her friend Lorraine were 'playing houses' in the big front dining room. When I went in at four o'clock to check that they were not suffering from hypothermia, I found them happily taking out every piece of cutlery from our wedding present canteen, and laying up the big table for a pretend reception for twelve people.

Just as Michael was going out to take a ward service at the hospital, Lorraine's mother came over to call her daughter over for tea. She said how nice it was that Lorraine and Pauline were such friends. She was obviously pleased that Lorraine's Sunday afternoons were being spent in such a safe environment as a vicarage. I shouted for the girls, who came tumbling out of the dining room giggling uncontrollably and with a faraway look in their eyes. There was an unmistakable smell of booze. The two mothers went into the dining room to retrieve Lorraine's coat, and there, on the table, was the incriminating evidence of our daughters' Sunday afternoon repast. Obviously the girls had not had taken 'afternoon tea at the vicarage'. They had taken out every wineglass we possessed and decanted the bottle of Harvey's Bristol Cream that the churchwarden had given us for Christmas. At the age of five Pauline and Lorraine could well be described as teetering on the 'drunk and disorderly'.

It was a wonder that any other children were in future allowed to play at the vicarage. Already it was a training ground for would-be arsonists and alcoholics!

Chapter Thirteen

Despite rumours among the adults of the neighbourhood about corruption at the vicarage, it was encouraging to know that children in our area still thought of it as a holy house. Walking to infants' school one day, with Pauline clutching my hand tightly, a little boy ran up to me and said 'Hello, Mrs God'. Feeling rather mystified at his greeting, but none the less elated, I asked how he knew my name.

'I've seen you with that man in black – the one who's always going in and out of church. I never knew his name till last week, but teacher said that church is God's house, so now I know. He must be God, and you're married to him, so you must be Mrs God.'

These words were a salutary reminder that although I couldn't claim to be God's wife, I was his child, and I was made in his likeness. I had a duty to try to become more like him.

Vicarage families are in the unenviable position of being 'watched' and this was particularly hard on children in school. They were expected to behave impeccably, and when they failed they were sometimes unfairly ridiculed and punished. 'We didn't expect it of a vicarage child.' Michael knew all about it, for he too was a vicarage child. I escaped such censure, but I did have to deal with people's expectations of what a vicar's wife should or should not do, and indeed what she should look like! I have yet to discover what a vicar's wife should look like, but I fear that the prototype involved lace-up shoes, fawn cardigans and woolly hats. Their actions should always include taking out calf's foot jelly to the sick of the parish, and of course serving precisely cut cucumber sandwiches to visiting bishops.

Intoxicating neighbours' children and dancing the can-can in fishnet tights at the parish party were certainly not on the 'perfect vicar's wife' agenda.

Certain of my other activities, however, did fit the bill, in many people's eyes. I hasten to add that I did them not to curry favour with God or man, but because I felt they were right for me, and hopefully would be helpful. They included being Enrolling Member of the Mothers' Union, Chair of the Ladies' section of the Bible Society, founder member of a spiritual dance-drama group, and roving reporter for the religious programme on Radio Leeds.

'Mrs God' was also seen to be useful in that she could play the organ, and fill in when necessary. I would recommend to all 'emergency organists' that they should learn to play *Jesu, joy of man's desiring* by heart. It is equally appropriate for weddings or funerals and can be elongated very easily, and also terminated quickly when the bride or the coffin arrives. If you are proficient on a two manual organ you can set the stops so that you can play the melody on one, and the underlying accompaniment more softly on the other. In a real emergency it is possible to keep the tune going using one hand only. I had proved this in dockland Hull, when playing an electronic organ, which was situated right in front of the pew where the groom and best man were seated. When it became obvious that they had had too much to drink and one of them was about to vomit, I managed to keep good old 'Jesu joy' going with one hand while using the other to remove the daffodils from the vase by the side of the organ and pass the receptacle to where it was urgently needed.

Only once did our brilliant Halifax organist fail to turn up on time for a service. It was the day of the Halifax Show – a large agricultural and horticultural show held on 'The Moor' opposite St. Jude's church and vicarage. The children and I had entered various cookery items and were waiting anxiously outside the marquee in sweltering sun, while the judges decided whether or not to award first prize for Mrs Walker's bread, Christopher's animal made out of a vegetable, and Pauline's Victoria sandwich cake. It was fortuitous that I happened to cast a glance over at the church just as a ribbon-bedecked bridal car arrived. I waited to see what the bridesmaids were wearing, and my attention was caught by a figure in white, waving frantically. It was not the bride. It was Michael, in surplice and white stole, looking very agitated.

I had to wait for a man to stamp my hand as a 'pass out' from the show, before braving the traffic on the crossroads to ascertain the reason for Michael's panic. It appeared that the organist had not turned up. With no time to collect any music from the vicarage I added greatly to the video being taken of the arriving guests, by calmly walking up the aisle wearing the briefest of shorts, and hoisting my bare legs over the organ stool in readiness for – yes you've guessed – *'Jesu, joy of man's desiring.'*

Meanwhile the organist was returning from a supermarket trip when he saw the bridal car stop in front of the church. Realising that he must have put the time down wrongly in his diary he parked as soon as he was able and gave the video man another memorable shot as he ran up the aisle at full pelt towards the organ. Giving me the greatest look of gratitude I had ever experienced, he shunted me up to the left hand side of the organ bench. As I continued to play the left hand soft accompaniment he calmly pulled out an oboe stop and proceeded to take over the melody with his right hand on the top manual. Johann Sebastian Bach had never heard his masterpiece played thus. Neither had a wedding congregation ever witnessed a female clad in short shorts bow in front of the altar on her way out through the lady chapel door seconds before Bach gave way to Wagner. Out goes the vicar's wife and here comes the bride. At least the congregation would not have known who I was; vicars' wives wear fawn cardigans and woolly hats!

Back at the vicarage I had a calming drink, then decided to get the dog lead and take Sheba over to the show. Of course she wasn't allowed in the cookery marquee, so I tied her up along with several other dogs that were lying flat out in the sun by the side of an adjacent stand from which issued an enticing aroma of onions. It was a serendipitous juxtaposition – a collection of panting canines under a banner proclaiming 'HOT DOGS'. I seized my camera, and captured the moment.

It had been a good day. Pauline and I had won trophies for our cookery, the organist had given me the whole of his wedding fee, and the following week I received a photographic voucher for the most original photo of Halifax show!

★★★★★★★★★★★★★★★

Sheba accepted the arrival of a baby in the vicarage with much more grace than she had accepted the arrival of Miss Picket's cockatiel. In fact she guarded Rosemary's pram with as much devotion to duty as a keeper of the crown jewels. Rosemary was at her most content when parked under the swaying branches of trees in the vicarage garden. Maybe this paved the way for her later career in forest conservation! She was also very fond of animals, and by the time she reached junior school age she was easy prey when her teacher asked for someone to look after the school gerbils during the long August break. St. Jude's vicarage was obviously viewed as an ideal holiday home for the two charming lady rodents from class 3.

Mrs Earnshaw may have been a good teacher, but sexing gerbils was not one of her talents. This became obvious by the end of August, when we had to go out and buy a new cage before there was a further gerbil population explosion.

'Please can we keep two of the babies, mummy?' the children pleaded.

'No –we've already got a dog and Miss Picket's squawking bird. '

'Please, daddy' implored Rosemary, who could always use her femininity and blue eyes to good effect with her father. He capitulated.

Before Christmas we had cause to be less critical of Mrs Earnshaw's sexing attempts. It was not easy. Our first attempt was unsuccessful. However, this December gerbil litter was at least well timed. There must be dozens of children just longing for gerbils for Christmas. How should we advertise our excess pets? Michael solved the problem by adding them to the church notices. After the reminders to the flower ladies, the request for magazine distributors and times of carol services, came an impassioned plea for buyers of vicarage-bred gerbils – a bargain at 25p. The following Sunday, with one gerbil down and three to go, the price was dropped to 20p. By Christmas Eve they were 'free to good home'.

The congregation was most tolerant, as over successive years the church notices included not only gerbils, but also hamsters from the vicarage breeding station.

Sheba continued to greet parishioners at the vicarage door with her unique toothless smile. She was prone to wandering down the back streets on a Sunday afternoon in the sure and certain hope of being given bones to gnaw at, from the remnants of parishioners' Sunday roasts. She grew too fat, so we tried to curb her wanderings, and just in case she slipped out into the back streets we had a label to hang round her neck. From the hospital where Michael was chaplain he acquired a notice, which stated 'NIL BY MOUTH'. It worked!

Sheba was a water fanatic and even before we inherited her she had ground down her teeth by diving to the seabed or riverbed to bring up huge stones in her mouth. I think she was crossed with a seal, for she could swim underwater for many yards, then bob up with her latest trophy of a rock. On one holiday in Aberystwyth we were joining in a holy Sunday evening 'Songs of Praise' with the local Salvation Army band on the promenade when we realised to our embarrassment that the singing was dwindling as people gravitated away from the service towards the railings. They were entranced by the dipping and diving of our aquatic Labrador, as she brought up progressively larger rocks to add to the cairn she was assembling on the beach.

Michael ran down to the beach to terminate our dog's 'playing to the gallery' and as the crowd returned to the hymn singing, the Salvation Army band struck up with a heartfelt rendition of 'Now thank we all our God.'

By the age of 16 Sheba was slowing down, was finding it more difficult to walk on her arthritic legs, and was developing an ominous lump. We knew we would have to make a decision soon, but put it off until after our annual holiday. That year we were going to the Isle of Wight. Michael got out of the car at Lymington to buy the ferry tickets, but unfortunately didn't realise he was within earshot of the children as he asked for two adults' and 3 children's return tickets but only a single ticket for a dog. He returned to a tearful family, who never forgave him for this indiscretion. Sheba had to be carried on her master's shoulders up and down the zigzag paths, but enjoyed a fortnight of sea-bathing and stone reclamation, and I do believe that when Michael had to pay out for another single ticket to Lymington, Sheba gave him a wry toothless grin!

Chapter Fourteen

A fortnight after returning from the Isle of Wight it was obvious that we must ask the vet 's opinion about prolonging Sheba's life. Michael waited in the car, but the tiny bit of optimism in his heart was immediately erased when I came out of the door carrying just a lead and a collar. Although Michael was able to remain professionally dry-eyed when conducting funerals of his parishioners, he could not turn off the tears when it came to his dog's death. I had to field the telephone calls for the next three days as the dog-owning members of the congregation phoned in with their condolences.

Five days later we had a family trip to the RSPCA in Halifax, where, from an unwanted litter, a black Labrador/cross puppy lolloped to the edge of the kennel and lifted up beseeching sky-blue eyes to Michael's matching ones. As his shiny black little body snuggled against Michael's black shirt and his tongue started to lick the white plastic dog collar, we knew that in a few minutes we would be in a pet shop buying another dog collar, and a matching lead.

There was no dispute about his name. Christopher, like his dad, was a railway enthusiast, and his current interest was in the Deltic class of locos. This dog must be called after one of the Deltic engines. It was important to have a name that was crisp enough to have venom injected into it when the situation demanded. 'Meld' and 'Crepello' were cast aside in favour of Pinza. So at the age of just seven weeks, Pinza joined the Walker family. He was so small that he fitted through a croquet hoop on our vicarage lawn, but he soon set the target of fattening himself up in record time. Weetabix seemed to be popular with the children, so presumably it was good for puppies. Unfortunately nobody had told him that two biscuits constituted the usual adult portion. We found him scarcely able to walk, with a hard distended tummy containing all but one Weetabix from a newly opened box. We had to prise off the remaining biscuit, which was stuck onto the roof of his greedy mouth. His already engorged gullet just could not hold any more!

Pinza ate hard, slept hard and played hard. One minute he could be a harmless soporific bundle, and the next he would have a mad session and chase around the room ready to leap and have a nibble with his needle-sharp teeth. One evening I left him sleeping in the lounge while I prepared refreshments for the church 'standing committee' due to have their meeting there at half past seven. Contrary to their title the standing committee do like to sit down for their meetings, so I had already set out eight chairs and tidied up – or at least I thought I had. By now the doorbell was ringing and Michael was taking people's coats into the cloakroom and urging the committee to take a seat in the lounge. On this occasion it appeared that the standing committee really was going to have to stand. The lounge furniture was tied together with green wool in a virtual spider's web, which was growing in front of their eyes. A demented Pinza was chasing round and round the chairs with the back of a knitted sweater which was diminishing rapidly as the wool unwound from my knitting needles.

The committee was re-routed to the dining room while I tried unsuccessfully to disentangle the spider's web and regretfully had to resort to scissors. Something had to be done about that fiendish dog. Worn out from his weaving Pinza was curled up in a ball, fast asleep. The unwritten words in the imaginary balloon said, 'Please don't be cross – it was such a good game!' I picked him up and gave him a cuddle before brewing the tea. Why do animals always win?

Like children they may give us grief from time to time, and try our patience, but they also have a great capacity for giving devotion and affection. Pinza seemed to tune in to our sadness when my mother died while on a visit to us. He would nuzzle his head into our laps and ooze out a generous stream of comfort when we most needed it.

Pinza was three when we moved from Halifax to Llangollen, where Michael had charge of six churches in the picturesque valley of the River Dee. He had calmed down a little, but his stealing capacity still knew no bounds. He had progressed from eating Weetabix to swallowing Christopher's ear pills. The vet recommended making him sick by giving him baking soda, but nothing would induce Pinza to eject what he had stealthily consumed. He never seemed to be any the worse for wear. Cucumber sandwiches, destined for the bishop's tea, had been put far back on the kitchen working surface, but with the flick of an extended paw they became an early afternoon meal for a hungry young dog. That was small fry by comparison with his later triumph of gnawing open the hamper containing a picnic for a visiting Bishop, wife and all our family, and devouring the chicken, rolls, salad, crisps and cake. All that remained was a half-eaten banana.

You would have thought that I would have learned to be more careful about where I put food. For twenty years I had lived in houses that had no central heating, and so I had never had a fridge. This was good news for opportunist dogs like Pinza. It was also a very busy household, and I always seemed to be working against the clock. I was never short on ideas – only short of time. Why did I once dream up the idea of serving rainbow biscuits along with the coffee after the Sunday school had performed songs from 'Noah'? Making the shortbread biscuits was easy. Icing them was not. Originally I had intended piping on them the seven different colours of the rainbow. After five minutes I reduced the colours to yellow, pink and a violent kingfisher blue.

I hoped the congregation would be impressed. Unfortunately they weren't. They never even saw my handiwork. It was hidden in the intestines of a dog with an insatiable appetite coupled with an ability to jump onto ever-higher cupboards.

The same fate awaited the Christingles. We had had a working party of ladies to adorn oranges with red ribbon (actually we used red insulating tape as this didn't slip) and to insert a candle into the top. The final stage was to put in four cocktail sticks, representing the four seasons. These were supposed to have fruits on them, but have you ever tried piercing raisins or sultanas? I come to grief when I try to pierce pineapple and cheese for parish buffets, so I had no qualms about substituting jelly babies for dried fruit on the Christingles. One prod through the tummy button area with one end of the stick, and a prod into the orange with the other end, and we soon had trays full of jolly Christingles.

I never knew until the following Sunday morning that dogs could open doors. Michael came down early in readiness for the 8 a.m. service to find a trail of dismembered oranges and a dog full of jelly-babies and broken ends of cocktail sticks. Maybe the gelatine coated Pinza's stomach and protected it from being pierced, for he suffered absolutely no ill effects. That afternoon I had to break my 'no shopping on the Sabbath' rule, hoping that my mother was not turning in her grave as I went out to buy more cocktail sticks and jelly babies to repair the damage before the evening service.

Pinza had one more attempt at being holy. This was the big time! Although he had once managed to open the dining room door he had obviously found it difficult. Far easier was to nudge open the sliding door of the study. We didn't worry unduly about this skill, as there were no consumables in the study as far as we could see. Obviously we did not see far enough.

The girls came in from school one day to be greeted by a black dog with a white nose. On the white circle stuck onto Pinza's nose was an embossed cross. In the study a newly delivered order of 500 communion wafers had been decimated. Not only were they impounded on his nose, but were aggravatingly stuck all over his large tongue. We could only laugh, and be grateful that he had taken communion in only one kind and, unlike Pauline at the age of five, had not progressed to the wine!

Chapter Fifteen

'There will be a meeting of the Mothers' Union on Wednesday afternoon at 2 p.m. and a famine lunch in aid of Ethiopia on Friday. A new booklet on our historic oak roof is available at the back of church for 50p and there are six gerbils at the bargain price of 25p.'

The congregations in our new parishes had not heard anything like this in church before!

We had arrived in Llangollen with a modest menagerie, comprising Pinza the dog, Smartie and Toffo the gerbils, together with their newly born family. With six churches in our parishes there were fresh fields for merchandising via the parish notices. With the infant gerbils rehoused, Rosemary felt it was now time to diversify. Florizel, our first hamster, moved into the vicarage in January 1985 – or should we say moved around it. Houdini was his middle name and his aim in life was to escape. He achieved his ambition in November 1985. Rosemary was understandably upset at his non-return from his latest excursions, and by now she was the last remaining child at home. Christopher was working for British Rail in

Willesden and Pauline had started at medical school in Cardiff.

Michael was anxious to compensate Rosemary, the last child in the nest, for the loss of Florizel, and acquiesced willingly to her request for a mouse. He agreed to buy one the next time he had to go to Shrewsbury. Before he reached the mouse section of the pet shop his attention was caught by a swiftly darting, beautiful striped creature in a large cage. It stopped for a moment on a branch and picked up a berry delicately in its paws, twisting it round until it found the juiciest side to eat. Michael ascertained that it was a chipmunk, that it would be happy to live alone, and would live many years longer than a mouse. Its price tag was also very much higher! However Michael had recently appeared on television on two of Harry Secombe's 'Highway' programmes filmed in Llangollen. He had enjoyed this experience immensely – especially being pampered by the make-up ladies who had had to powder his bald head before each shoot, as it reflected the lights too much. For his appearances he was paid £50. Shrewsbury pet shop was grateful; Michael returned home with a chipmunk, and was determined to build it a big cage where it would have a much happier life than being stuck in a shop window.

I returned home to find Michael sawing a wooden packing case, and fixing a wire front to make a home for Crepello (a.k.a. *wiwer* which is the Welsh for squirrel). Released from its box the chipmunk seized its chance to gain freedom and scurried along the landing into Rosemary's bedroom. But where was it now? Nowhere to be seen. It must be under the bed. In lifting the divan bed onto its side and resting it against the wall we had done a terrible thing. We had crushed the unfortunate little animal that now lay flattened, with its legs splayed out. I had always steered well clear of steam rollers because my dad had said if I got under one it would make me so flat that they would be able to post me under the door.

Banishing such thoughts I ushered Rosemary out of the room and lifted the chipmunk into its cage, which I covered with a dark cloth, feeling like a judge donning his black cap before issuing the death sentence. Yet something inside me said I should not interfere any more, but let nature take its course. I was due to serve tea at the interval at a concert in church so I left Christopher, who was conveniently home for a few days, comforting Rosemary. Kneeling at the back of church during the penultimate choral piece I prayed earnestly once more to St. Francis and to St. Jude and to the creator of all life, including striped chipmunks, courtesy of Harry Secombe. Returning home and expecting to be met by two mourners I had a heavy heart as I opened the vicarage door. But I was greeted with shouts of delight. Upstairs, admiring her new cage was an inflated animal, who seemed to have no after effects from her squashing.

Thereafter we decided that the best place for her to run around in safety would be the bathroom, so there she lived for several years in her mansion of a cage, being let out at bath time when she would run up and down the curtains and then perch on the towel rail to contemplate the weird naked humans enjoying their water play. Michael's father had never been converted to becoming an animal lover, and he froze at the sight of a chipmunk living in the bathroom.

However long his stay with us, Grandpa never had a bath, preferring to wash and shave in the kitchen.

Our range of rodents eventually extended to a white mouse and various hamsters, one of which was Hermit who developed a cancerous eye. Sandra the vet was doubtful about his ability to survive, but as she was keen to try operating on such a tiny animal she offered to remove the offending eye. I had thought she was acting on the previous morning's reading in church 'If thine eye offend thee pluck it out...' but she assured me it was just that she wanted the challenge of intricate surgery, and that if the hamster didn't pull through then she wouldn't charge. On Tuesday morning the phone went. Good news! I don't know who was the most pleased – Sandra the vet, Rosemary or me. Hermit not only survived, but also took on a new lease of life and enjoyed two more energetic one-eyed years.

Meanwhile his white furry friend Ambrose (born on St. Ambrose's day) had the Houdini streak in him and went missing for several days, causing great distress. Eventually we heard scratching in the bathroom; it was not from the chipmunk, but seemed to come from the airing cupboard. Rosemary insisted that her dad should lift up the floorboards, which necessitated judicious removal of the lino. Yes – there was a definite rustling. He was down there somewhere, but was not going to show his face yet. We played the waiting game. It wasn't only Grandpa who couldn't have a bath; nobody could. The bathroom floor was out of action, and Michael was perturbed to receive a letter advising us of the imminent arrival of the diocesan parsonage board inspector. He would undoubtedly want to view the bathroom. With one day to spare Ambrose came up for air, and was captured underneath an upturned waste paper basket. His white fur was now dirty grey, and had to be attacked with a clothes brush, after we had written off, as foolhardy, the idea of applying the vacuum hose. He was so curious he would have poked his head in the nozzle and been sucked up to Hoover heaven.

Jenny, our curate, was a frequent caller at the vicarage; she was very friendly to Rosemary, who had once been to her Diocesan Youth camp, but she was less than keen on Rosemary's animals. When Rosemary diversified to keeping rats I really thought Jenny might say goodbye to parish ministry in Llangollen.

'Please tell your daughter not to answer the door with two rats on her shoulder' she pleaded. 'Those long straggly tails make me feel ill.'

Thereafter we tried to ensure that Andreas and Christoph, the rats, were firmly in their cage when visitors came. They got on well together. This was not surprising, as once again the experts had got it wrong gender-wise. The result was a brood of eleven baby rats two weeks before the Mothers' Union Christmas party at the vicarage. Their cage was situated at the end of the passage next to the toilet. When they heard footsteps approaching they all leapt onto the cage door and peered out, swaying their long tails in unison. We found it delightful, but feared the Mothers' Union ladies would not share our enthusiasm, so we covered the cage up with a large tablecloth, and tried to persuade any toilet-seekers to go to the upstairs loo. Until we heard Mrs Jones screaming we had forgotten that the ladies would go into the bathroom to wash their hands, and be petrified by a bounding chipmunk. Ambrose the hamster was on one of his bi-monthly walkabouts, but mercifully did not reappear in ghostly form from the airing cupboard. This really would have jeopardised all my efforts to increase the Mothers' Union branch membership!

The following month I answered the door to a lady I didn't recognise, but whose mellifluous voice seemed familiar.

'I hear that you look after people's animals while their owners are away. Could you manage two dogs for a week?'

I assured her that she must have misunderstood. We had a dog, a chipmunk, several rats, a mouse and two hamsters – that was quite enough.

'But I copied your address down from the little card in the paper shop' she insisted. She handed over the slip which read, *'Going on holiday – anxious about your pets? A good home awaits at Llangollen Vicarage, Abbey Road, where I will give them every care. Moderate rates. Rosemary Walker '*

Bowled over by this disclosure, but secretly pleased at my younger daughter's business acumen, I asked for more details about the lady's dogs.

'Oh – they're not mine. They are my daughter's. I'm June Knox-Mawer, by the way, and my daughter, who's an actress, has to go to London for a week. The hotel managers are used to having her Labrador, but are not keen on having two puppies who are not house-trained.'

Neither was I, but I knew Rosemary would be cross at losing her first customer – June Knox-Mawer, no less - a well-known broadcaster. So it was that two delightful puppies, Rosie and Blodwen came for their holidays. Pinza was very tolerant as long as they didn't sleep on his beanbag or play with his ball. Michael and I were pretty tolerant too, although it did mean that when anyone came to the vicarage door we not only had to throw a tablecloth over the rats, check that nobody went into the bathroom, see that Ambrose was securely in his cage, but also had to run for the mop and disinfectant. As I removed evidence of incontinent puppies from our rather fine tiled hall floor, Michael picked up the plump little puppies and answered the door. By that time most visitors had decided we were out and had gone on their way.

The Diocesan Parsonage board inspector paid us a surprise February visit, bearing instructions on how to look after our famous Ruabon patterned tiles. Living in a 'free' vicarage has many advantages. On the other hand one was always subject to strange regulations. In one diocese I was severely reprimanded for letting the painter use turquoise paint on the outside of the house. Apparently it had to be stipulation Oxford Blue.

'Don't let it happen again' I was warned. I felt like a third former about to be sent to detention. I had been going to ask for a new kitchen ceiling, but dared not push my luck. When the inspector saw the loose polystyrene ceiling tile he would surely see the need for a new ceiling. Or would he?

'I'll leave you six nails – I'm sure your husband can tap them in, and they'll hold the tile up.'

And now I was being lectured on my floor cleaning techniques.

'I just can't understand why some of the tiles are coming loose' said the inspector.

'Are you sure you don't flood them with water?'

He looked menacingly at me. I knew he would not believe me when I said that I didn't.

At that point I heard Michael's car crunch up the gravel drive, and with a bang of the back door he came through the kitchen and into the hall through the interlocking door. Out bounded Blodwen and Rosie. As they looked up at the glowering inspector Blodwen took perfect aim at his shoes. The vicarage tiles were now gleaming in their wetness, and as the inspector receded, banging the front door behind him with a resounding bang, the dithering tile dropped off the kitchen ceiling!

Chapter Sixteen

Ferrero Rocher boxes – the transparent rigid plastic ones – are ideal for keeping things in. I hoard such containers and vow to fill them in an organised fashion with paperclips, drawing pins, or pencils and dice for parish parties. Until Trinity Sunday in 1987 I had never thought of them as caskets for burials.

Michael had preached on the difficult concept of the Holy Trinity, using a three-pronged plug as a visual aid, and we finished the service with 'Holy, holy, holy, Lord God Almighty'. Leaving Michael to continue his hand-shaking outside the church door I went up the path, looking firstly back at the Horseshoe Falls and then towards the lych-gate where Rosemary and her school friend Marcia were greeting the emerging congregation.

'Has Dad finished yet?' asked Rosemary.
'We want him for the burial' added Marcia.
Mrs Keynes, the churchwarden's wife was unaware of an interment after Mattins.
'Who's died, then?' she asked.

'It's Maybelle' they replied very solemnly.

'Is Mabel your auntie?'

'Oh no – she's our brain-damaged rat. Would you like to see her?'

Before Mrs Keynes could turn away, the girls uncovered the Ferrero Rocher box, which held the cadaver of the late Maybelle – their jointly owned white rat.

'Sorry she looks a bit funny, but we had to break her back to fit her in the box as rigor mortis had set in.'

By now the rest of the flock were in on this gruesome conversation. It was all they needed to hear just before their Sunday lunch.

Luckily Michael emerged from the back door of the church at this point so I encouraged the girls to take their request and their casket to him, while I soothed the reeling ladies, and guided them out of the churchyard before Maybelle was laid to rest by the wall under a hastily made wooden cross, and given a reverent, paternal blessing.

As soon as I got home I made a note in my diary: - *Do not give Mr & Mrs Keynes Ferrero Rocher chocolates for Christmas.*

My track record of dealing with churchwardens and their wives had taken yet another dip. In our first incumbency Michael and I were determined to practise hospitality (as encouraged by St. Paul) so decided to have informal buffet suppers for a dozen randomly picked members of our congregation. Firstly, however, we felt we should invite the vicar's warden and his wife to dinner. The latter was a *cordon bleu* cook, and even now I cringe at the memory of the very dry, overcooked chicken that I served up. Any hopes of restoring faith in their new incumbent's wife by serving a reasonably elegant pineapple pudding, was blown away when the church clock chimed and struck eight o'clock.

Coming from Beverley with two of its fine churches, St. Mary's and the Minster, having wonderful, finely tuned bells, I had been disappointed to find no ring of bells in any of the churches in Michael's first three parishes. This last one did have clock bells, but the timing on the chimes was set wrongly, and the musical interval between the chimes and the striking hour bell was horrifically weird.

I cringed involuntarily as the clock started to ring out at eight, and most unwisely asked 'can anything be done about those awful bells?'

I feared that the noise of Michael's scraping chair, which accompanied a hefty kick to my ankles, did not obscure my question. I feared correctly. The warden and his wife drank their coffee during an uneasy silence. After their premature departure from the vicarage Michael showed me the parish guidebook. Guess who had been the generous donor of those awful bells?

We fared somewhat better with another warden and his wife in that same parish. In fact the warden and I exchanged smiles in the side aisle each Sunday. Philip was an excellent warden, but was quite shy and was very embarrassed when the idea of 'giving the peace' was introduced into the Communion service. He did not want to shake hands, let alone be embraced by overpowering women. Therefore, on the pretext of being near the door to welcome latecomers, he positioned himself at the back of the side aisle. I was a 'side-aisler' for a different reason. It was easier to control three children there, rather than in the middle of a hundred pair of eyes, some of which were less than compassionate if the vicarage children misbehaved. So each Sunday morning while those in the main aisle were wishing each other peace, Philip and I did it discreetly, with just a knowing little nod and smile.

We were pleased to be invited to his house for a party on the day after Boxing Day. Michael picked us up after doing a home communion, and as we got out of the car he confessed that he had caught his surplice in the door and that it was covered with oil. The warden's wife broke off from her cooking to spray the surplice and then put it into soak. We sat down to a good Yorkshire spread, and were just looking forward to playing games with their family when Pauline's face turned to the shade of green so well known to all parents of carsick children. She didn't make it to the toilet, but deposited her tea over the warden's brand new carpet – his Christmas gift to his wife.

This good lady was already reaching for a different stain removal bottle and together we sprayed and scrubbed the carpet.

It was blatantly obvious that we needed to get Pauline home to bed, so with profuse apologies we made our premature farewells. It was unfortunate that they let us out of their front door. We had entered by the back. Snow was falling as Christopher ran on ahead, and disappeared from view. We were still in the kitchen wringing out the oily surplice when Christopher sloshed his way in, snow on his head, mud on his best shoes and pondweed on his trousers. Philip hadn't warned us of the frozen goldfish pond.

His wife came through from her carpet cleaning operation, handed us the can of oil-removing spray together with a wet surplice, and said, somewhat wearily, that she didn't have anything that would work on pondweed. The following Sunday Philip was in the main aisle. He said it was his new year's resolution to come to terms with the 'peace' in the new service, but I had an inkling that he felt this might be an easier option than smiling at the vicar's wife who had wrought such havoc at his Christmas party!

By the time we moved into the next parish I was well on the way to eligibility for Mastermind, with my specialist subject being *embarrassing moments.*

As Education and Media representative for the Diocesan Mothers' Union I was asked to write and direct a road show, which would present the work of the organisation in a light-hearted, but meaningful way. This I did in the form of a sketch based on Cilla Black's television show, *Blind Date,* casting our amenable bishop's wife in the role of Cilla. This road show was presented at several venues from the north Wales coast down to rural Montgomeryshire and seemed to go down well. After the final performance I was called onto the stage along with the actresses to take my bow, as producer. As I waited in the wings for my cue I caught the heel of my shoe in some sacking. Ripping it off I saw that the sacking was part of the trappings of a bunch of dusty pink and blue cloth artificial flowers. I dislike artificial flowers of any kind and thought this rather drab affair quite hideous. Obviously it had been a prop in the previous week's pantomime in the church hall. I gave it a well-deserved kick into the bowels of the backstage.

After I had glowed with satisfaction at the kind words said about the production I was aware of a hiatus in the proceedings. Then I heard a scrabbling noise backstage. They had lost the presentation bouquet. I knew exactly where it was, but I wasn't going to let on. I put on a hypocritically brave face, and trotted out the usual 'it's the thought that counts' with overdone vicar's wife's charm. The audience clapped. I made a hasty exit – but not before the Deanery Presiding Member had run out into the car park with an exultant 'we've found it – sorry it's a bit dusty and squashed. I'm sure you can restore it.'

I did. It was my daughter's birthday coming up, and it would look lovely in her kitchen!

I was a bit late for the next Mothers' Union Diocesan Council meeting in Wrexham, so I crept in and sat at the back. Busily taking notes about the proposed project for the year I paused to sign my name at the bottom of a list on a clipboard that was being passed round. I was relieved that I had arrived in time to sign in.

It is customary at Mothers' Union meetings to pause for midday prayers. After remembering our linked dioceses in Uganda and Australia we were asked to remember those who were ill. Finally we were bidden to stand for a minute's silence in memory of those who had died. From her clipboard the secretary read out their names:

Millicent Brown

Mary Jones

and …*(sharp intake of breath)…,* Margaret Walker.

There was a gasp of disbelief from the assembled company, followed by a babble of chatter. I sat there, mesmerised for a moment, wondering what to do.

'Actually I'm here; I'm still alive' I called out from the back row, noting with some pleasure the relief on people's faces.

I shall not be around to read my obituary, but I still relish the memory of that heart-warming gasp at the self-inflicted false news of my death.

My schoolteacher used to instil into me, 'Margaret, read the question!'

My university tutor had warned me, 'Margaret, look more carefully at your exam timetable!'

Now I say to myself, 'Margaret, look more carefully at what you are signing. It could be your death warrant!'

Chapter Seventeen

Pinza, who had been born on a rough housing estate in Halifax, had spent ten happy years enjoying canal and river walks in Llangollen in between eating cucumber sandwiches, the bishop's picnic, Christingles and communion wafers. Now he was to sample even more rural life in mid Wales when we moved to live in the welcoming village of Kerry in 1993. Over the next two years he started to slow down, but something was to happen that would change his life.

By 1995 the children had left home – at least for the time being! Christopher was working for British Rail in Warrington; Pauline had qualified as a doctor and was now a clinical physician engaged in medical research, and Rosemary – who now preferred to be called Rosie – was working three miles away from us in Newtown, as Wales Wildlife and Countryside Link Officer. She now had her own little house and would love to have had a dog, but felt it unwise as she was out at work all day.

When Sue, the local vet rang Rosie with a sob story about an unwanted border collie who had been left tied up on the surgery door, Rosie listened sympathetically, but said she couldn't help, as by now she had acquired a cat. Was it Sue or Rosie, or both, who thought of ringing us? It was clear that the vets couldn't keep this 10-month-old bitch, and unless they could find her a home she would have to be put down. Heartstrings were duly pulled and we agreed to drive into Newtown to view this orphan. The assistant unbolted the cage and out tumbled a pretty black and white border collie who immediately rolled on her back, with legs in the air, and pleaded with her limpid eyes for mercy and a loving home.

We decided to have her on trial for the morning to see if she and Pinza were compatible. The minute she jumped into the car Pinza woke from his sleep and immediately regained his adolescent vivacity. When we let them both out in Hafren forest they ran off, splashed in the river and played as if they had been friends for life.

We had no idea of the new dog's name. We tried sheepdog names – *Meg, Bess,* and *Tess,* but there was no sign of recognition. We tried her with Welsh and English commands, to no avail, though she did come to us when we whistled. Starting on a new round of possible names I came to *Rhian.* Her ears pricked and she obviously approved. We returned via the vets' surgery, paid a nominal amount as a purchase price and a significantly higher price for the necessary injections.

Pinza was eternally grateful for this pretty bitch who enlivened his last weeks. It was useful to have Rhian to paw his face when she heard our car approaching. It gave him just enough time to roll off the forbidden settee, thereby saving him from his master's wrath. We too were grateful for Rhian's timely arrival. Training a new young dog helped to fill the void when Pinza's 15 years of memorable living were over.

We enrolled at a dog training class. This was wrongly timed as Rhian came on heat and did not concentrate on commands when she had the attention of so many dogs. A handsome golden retriever whose owner was another vicar's wife was especially interested. Rhian was so inattentive that the fearsome training lady pulled her into the centre of the circle where the other owners were performing flawless walks, turns, sits and stays. She gave me Rhian's lead and made me walk, dog-less, in the circle.

'That will make Rhian so embarrassed that she'll be keen to cooperate', said the trainer.

Guess who was embarrassed? It certainly was not Rhian! She lay down in a relaxed pose while her red-faced owner walked, reversed, and ordered imaginary dogs to sit and stay. At the end of the 10 lessons we all received certificates. I was thrilled. Only when the other vicar's wife and I compared our yellow ones with the others' blue ones did we realise that ours said 'For attendance'. The blue certificated dogs undoubtedly went on to win Crufts' agility tests or learned to dance the foxtrot. Ours returned home happily to resume vicarage life.

Michael and I still cast blame on each other for what happened early one Sunday morning. Yes, I admit that I had felt sorry for the muddy, bedraggled farm dog who had taken up his stance outside our back door. In fact I had given him some biscuits and even put an old coat for him to sleep on in our garage. Yet it was Michael who had not checked whether the back door had clicked shut while he was packing up the car in readiness for his three Sunday morning services. As I looked out of the dining room window I saw a flash of black and white in the field, and realised that Rhian had gone. So had the farm dog. We raced round in the car to *Mucky Lane* but were too late to intercept. Monday morning saw us at the library asking for books on dog whelping.

As the expected delivery date drew closer Michael started to convert my old kitchen cabinet into a whelping box. Rhian started pawing nervously in a corner. Our phone was out of order so Michael went to borrow next-door's mobile in case we needed the vet. I could see Michael and Brendan walking to a spot where they could get a signal. Their wanderings were in vain. So was the whelping box. Rhian had calmly produced the first of her six puppies on the doormat in our front porch. She was not for budging from this delivery suite, so we instructed the postman and parishioners to use the back door for the next two months. The mop and bucket were once again in use. The vet warned us of further mess after the puppies were wormed. This did not worry us. We were off to the Holy Land for 10 days to lead a deanery pilgrimage. In his Christmas letter cousin John had volunteered to dog-sit Rhian. We broke it to him gently that he would have the joy of 4-week old puppies, who had just been wormed, and promised to pray for him in all the holy churches we visited in Palestine.

Finding homes for the puppies was initially no problem. We were sad to see them go, but Rhian was glad. She had been a marvellous mother, but she had her own life to lead.

A fortnight later the nice couple who had taken Tessa and Sophie rang to say that the man was proving allergic to dogs. They had found Tessa a good home as a working dog on a farm near Carno, but would have to bring Sophie back. Rhian was not amused. The following week our organist drove up in her Land Rover clutching a writhing energetic bundle. It was Bonzo, the macho puppy.

'I just can't cope with this dog' she said.

'He's terrorising all the other dogs on the farm, and he's just jumped up and ripped all my washing off the line.'

Rhian's puppies had, like the gerbils, already been tagged onto the end of church notices. We needed a new area of approach. On a post-Easter visit to our Porthmadog cottage we were in luck. Two of our Welsh-speaking neighbours were wanting dogs; so Sophie became Soffi, and Bonzo became Sion. We see these dogs daily now and are pleased to report that they are a tribute to their wayward parents.

Returning to our parishes after that Easter, Michael decided to organise a 'service of talents' at Llanmerewig church. The congregation was asked to bring to church a token of one of their talents, which they were using in the service of the church or community. These offerings were collected on a large plate and blessed, by Michael, at the altar. He then proceeded to base his sermon about these diverse items.

Dorothy, our worship leader, was an artist. Her offering was a palette and paintbrush.

Pat arranged flowers and added secateurs to the plate. Margaret, well known for her culinary delights put on a wooden spoon. Peter, the treasurer was an auctioneer, who often used his gifts to raise money for charity, so he put onto the plate his gavel.

The mound of talents was so high by the time the plate came to me that I could only just find room for the sheet of music bearing a hymn, which I had composed. To stop it blowing away, Aileen, the Sunday school teacher, anchored it with a heavy metal object, which looked like a cross between an adjustable spanner and a pair of nutcrackers.

Michael was doing well, I thought, weaving all these items into his talents sermon. It would have been invidious to leave anyone out, but I could see that he was struggling when it came to the shiny metal contraption. Waving it high in the pulpit he ploughed on with a nebulous spiel relating to Aileen's talent.

'I'm sure Aileen is very adept at using this' he said. The congregation giggled.

'It's a wonder she has time to do any craft work, with a sheep farm and three young children'.

By now there was rolling in the pews, and laughter, that could not be constrained.

Before Michael went further into the mire I ascertained from the farmer sitting in front of me the function of the mystery object.

It was a castration device.

I was tempted to shout 'Cut' to stop Michael rambling on, but fearing this would further add to the mirth, I coughed loudly instead. Michael took the hint and brought the sermon to a swift conclusion.

I've just done the reading from Romans 12 at the Women's World Day of Prayer service. *We have different gifts* said St. Paul. He goes on about teaching, encouraging, giving, leading, governing and showing mercy and serving. I think of Aileen. *'They also serve who only stand and snip'*

★★★★★★★★★★★★★★★

A good shepherd moves his flock around from time to time to graze on fresh pasture. So, in 2001, we moved west to our retirement cottage above Porthmadog harbour from where we can gaze towards the sea, marvel at the Moelwyn mountains and follow the progress of the trains on the Ffestiniog railway.

While we are enjoying having more time to pursue existing hobbies of music, model making, photography and gardening, we have ventured into new fields. Michael has unleashed a talent for bread making. Tap dancing has turned from my dream to a reality, and I have found a new enjoyment in circle dancing. On the windowsill stands a pair of vases, fashioned in clay by my own fair hands. These are a daily reminder of what can be achieved if you take the plunge and tackle something outside your normal comfort zone.

As you face the reality of the recession you may have to think seriously of what fresh approaches you might have to take. You may even have to forego your Sunday roast and tackle a recipe from *Margaret's Million Ways with Mince.* I could also recommend delicious dishes made from ox tail, pigs' trotters and lambs' hearts. However I am sure that by now you will be inspired to tap into your own wells of creativity, and be eager to devise your own imaginative dishes. Together we could update our wartime recipe books and add *Recessionary rissoles, Frugal faggots, and Crispy credit crunchies.*

So, be innovative. Experiment with unusual ingredients. But whatever you do:

DON'T EAT THE CAT!